Windows Server 2012: A Handbook for Professionals

By Aditya Raj

Published By

Aditya Raj has been serving IT sector as a hardware, network and system engineer since completed his post graduation, Master of Science in Computer Networking from the University of Bedfordshire (United Kingdom).

He is currently working with KDDI India PVT LTD and supporting NIKON India network infrastructure which includes routers, switches, firewalls and MS servers. He has designed, implemented and managed systems running windows Server 2008 R2, SQL Server 2008 R2 and Dynamics NAV 2009 SP1. In contemporary time, he is supporting Windows server 2012, MSSQL 2012 and Dynamics NAV 2013 R2. Moreover, he has also configured SharePoint 2010, 2013 and Dynamics CRM 2011, 2013.

He has earned various certifications which includes Microsoft Certified Solutions Associate (MCSA), Microsoft Certified Professional (MCP) and Cisco Certified Network Associate (CCNA).

He has already contributed in book publication through his book title "*MOSH: A New Era of Remote Access*" that is published on Amazon.

Preface

"Windows Server 2012: A Handbook for Professionals" is based on author's professional journey especially at KDDI India PVT LTD, India. It technically as well as professionally elaborates all topics of Microsoft Server environment, however, does not follow the style and format of a text book. Readers are expected to be quite familiar with the fundamentals of Computer Networking. This book aids the windows server administrators and professionals to understand high level approach, edifice on their existing knowledge and also broaden their server concept which is needed for the server 2012.This book illustrates the expertise and knowledge essential for implementing, maintaining, managing and provisioning infrastructure and services in server 2012. IT professionals who have knowledge of windows server 2012 operating system should consider this book a supplement as it covers the real world experiences and scenarios. Some topics which are discussed in this book are not strictly under the networking/server domains. Moreover, please visit MSDN, TechNet, Blogs and forms if you are not comfortable with contains which are mentioned in this book.

You can reach to the author at below e-mail address.

Aditya Raj

adityaraj_sharma@yamil.com

Acknowledgment

I would like to convey my ardent admiration and gratitude to **Mr. Naoki Nohira** for his immense help, support and inspiration for my book both professionally and personally. Without his supervision and assistance, completing this book would not have been achievable.

I am also very obliged for the continuous assistance which I received from my family and friends especially **Ramyani Das and Mansi Jain** during this vigorous period.

I would like to contribute this book to my parents for their enormous support towards me and my book. I really feel honored for their unconditional inspiration and assistance for enlighten me to the correct path.

TABLE OF CONTENT

Chapter 1

Introduction, Capabilities & Features

Objectives

The following objectives are covered in this chapter:

- Server 2012 capabilities, features and editions.
- Planning for server 2012 in existing infrastructure.
- Server 2012 roles, H/W requirements and up-gradation path.
- Interfaces of server 2012.
- Migration preparation and tools.
- Enlighten on NIC Teaming.

Introduction

This chapter elucidates the Server 2012 in terms of three key components – planning, installation and configuration. These components pave the beginning way for an administrator to know what you are going to be installing. Moreover, need to gather the requirements about the edition and hardware requirements. It is also necessary to know about what you are going to end up with and most important one should actually knows how to perform this installation. Another question arises wither it is a server core installation or a standard installation.

Even you complete the installations still there are certain things which are tentative. For instance, maybe you start server core installation and then you change it over to a full installation, or maybe you need to migrate some of the options and roles that were available in a previous edition, like Server 2008 over to your 2012 environment. Thus, planning is very imperative during installation and configuration of server 2012.

1.1: Windows Server 2012 Capabilities

There are six main capabilities of windows server 2012 which has shown as below.

1. Virtualization
2. Networking and remote access
3. Identity and security
4. Storage, Availability and Server Management
5. Web and application platform
6. Features on demand

Now, need to kind of delve a little deeper about these different capabilities that Windows Server 2012 has to offer to us.

1.1.1: Server Virtualization

1. Secure isolated tenants (Server roles).
2. Supports up to 64 virtual CPSs, A TB of memory and 4000 VMs.

3. Incremental backup support.

4. Resource metering, offloaded data transfer, quality of service.

5. Live migration.

6. Hyper-V replication to offsite locations in the network or the cloud.

7. Failover.

8. SMB shares for virtual storage.

1.1.2: Networking and Remote Access

1. Automation and consolidation of networking processes and resources.

2. Easy connection of private clouds with public clouds.

3. Seamless connection to IT resources and services spanning physical boundaries and cloud environments.

4. Network appears as single server.

5. Automatic rerouting maintains server uptime.

6. Virtual desktop infrastructure pools desktop and remote sessions.

1.1.3: Identity and Security

1. Active directory rights management services – protect documents from being unencrypted, printed or forwarded.

2. Dynamic access control – Tag data to utilize access policies.

3. Simplified active directory deployment.

4. Clone virtualized domain controllers.

5. Automatically, generate powershell scripts for directory control.

6. Improved powerShell.

1.1.4: Storage, Availability and Server Management

1. Eliminate users' disruptions during maintenance.

2. Isolate unexpected problems before they occur.

3. Improved storage, performance, server and networking technologies.

4. Deploy workloads to remote and virtual disks.

5. Multi server environment that can be configured and managed remotely.

6. Single integrated server manager console to manage all servers.

1.1.5: Web and Application Platform

1. Windows Azure service bus.

2. Windows Azure connects.

3. Virtual machine portability.

4. Same development tools for server 2012 and azure.

5. Open platform - .Net, PHP, Node.js, Python< HTML5, WebSockets.

6. Better provisioning.

7. Better SSL scalability.

8. Host web based application locally or in the cloud.

1.1.6: Features on Demands

It means swapping of server 2012 from GUI to server core and vice-versa. You are not stuck with server core if you change your mind and you want a graphical installation. You can upgrade it later to a full graphical environment or a minimum graphical environment. You have an in-between level if you want as well, a Minimal Server Interface. Thus, there is more flexibility in server core than we used to be. Because of an option called *Features on Demand* that will actually allow you to fully uninstall even the binaries of particular features. So, it can't be installed without going out of your way and going back to the media to finalize that installation, and that actually keeps the system even cleaner. Hence, Server Core – if you looked that in 2008 or 2008 R2 and dismissed it because of some issues with it, definitely give it a look again. This may be the installation option as you want.

1.2: Evaluate Server 2012 Needs for Existing Infrastructure

Evaluation based on three major facts which are as below.

1. Business case.
2. Current environment.
3. Licensing.

Moreover, there is some things you definitely want to think about, and process through, and work with the other shareholders, and that are a part of your environment to make sure that you are delivering exactly what you're promising, and may able to provide the technologies that are going to make your business run that much more smoothly. So, you need to figure out some questions before implementing the server 2012 in an organization.

1. An organization really ready for this whole Server 2012 thing?
2. Does company need it?
3. Is it going to be useful for the organization?

1.2.1: Plan for Server Roles and Capacities in Server 2012

Microsoft Assessment and Planning Toolkit is something you may want to consider for downloading. The *Microsoft Assessment and Planning Toolkit* or *MAP* gives you the ability to inventory, which you currently have in terms of operating systems, hardware, and software in your network. And it will allow you to observe following requirements.

What are your current needs?

1. Existing server roles.
2. Existing capacity.
3. Existing network and physical infrastructure.
4. Peak workload.
5. Bottlenecks.

Determine your readiness for Win server 2012 & Win 8

1. Migrates your VMware-based virtual machine to hyper – V.
2. Size your server environment for desktop virtualization.
3. Simplify migration to SQL server 2012.
4. Evaluate your licensing needs for Lync 2010.
5. Determine active users and devices.

Windows Assessment and Planning Toolkit (MAP)

The Microsoft Assessment and Planning Toolkit or MAP gives you the ability to inventory which you currently have in terms of operating systems, hardware and software in your network. This may be the tool that you use that allows you to really get a complete picture of what is going on in your network, what the edges of your network, what kind of performance areyou getting in your network, and thereby be able to start the process of making that transition of all or some of your server based infrastructure to server 2012.

1.3: Windows Server 2012 Editions

1. Windows server 2012 Standard.
2. Windows server 2012 Datacenter.

NOTE: - Windows server 2012 does not come in enterprise edition.

1.4: Windows Server 2012 Roles

1. Active Directory Certificate Services (AD DC).
2. Active Directory Domain Services (AD DS).
3. Active Directory Federation Services (AD FS).
4. Active Directory Lightweight Directory Services (AD LDS).
5. Active Directory Right Management Services (AD RMS).
6. Application Server.

7. DHCP Server.

8. DNS Server.

9. Group Policy.

10. Hyper –V.

11. IP Address Management.

12. Network Load Balancing.

13. Networking.

14. Print and Document Services.

15. Remote Desktop Services.

1.5: Windows Server 2012 Minimum Hardware Requirements

1. 2.4 GHz, 64-bit CPU (does not support 32 bit and itanium processors)

2. 512 MB RAM

3. 32 GB free hard disk

4. Super VGA (800x600) display resolution

5. A network connection

NOTE: - To know the system requirements, you can use Microsoft planning tool kit. In addition, you can also use windows memory diagnostics tool.

1.6: Windows Server 2012 Upgrade Path

Let's talk about upgrading for a moment and about the different editions that are available in Server 2012. Table 1.1 and 1.2, show the up-gradation path from server 2008 and 2008 R2 respectively.

Table 1.1: Windows Server 2012 upgrade path.

Windows Server 2008 Edition	Can be upgraded to
Windows Server 2008 Standard with SP2	Windows Server 2012 Standard or Windows Server 2012 Datacenter
Windows Server 2008 Enterprise with SP2	Windows Server 2012 Standard or Windows Server 2012 Datacenter
Windows Server 2008 Datacenter with SP2	Windows Server 2012 Datacenter
Windows Web Server 2008	Windows Server 2012 Standard

Table 1.2: Windows Server 2012 upgrade path.

Windows Server 2008 R2 Edition	Can be upgraded to
Windows Server 2008 R2 Standard with SP1	Windows Server 2012 Standard or Windows Server 2012 Datacenter
Windows Server 2008 R2 Enterprise with SP1	Windows Server 2012 Standard or Windows Server 2012 Datacenter
Windows Server 2008 R2 Datacenter with SP1	Windows Server 2012 Datacenter
Windows Web Server 2008 R2	Windows Server 2012 Standard

NOTE: - SQL server 2012 can run on windows server 2012 core version. Before that it was not supported in previous core versions.

1.7: Advantages of Server Core Installation

1. Reduces disk space.
2. Reduces potential attack space.
3. Reduce servicing requirements.
4. Default installation.

1.8: Advantages of Server with GUI

1. Familiar Windows interface.
2. Graphical management tools.

1.9: Minimal Server Interface

1. It is an option to install Server with a GUI and then remove the Server Graphical Shell.
2. It is approximately 300 MB smaller than Server with a GUI mode.
3. The Server Code mode is approximately 4 GB smaller than Server with a GUI mode.
4. For the smallest possible disk consumption, begin with a Server Core installation and completely remove unneeded server role or features.

Reference Table to Compare Features

Table 1.3: Windows Server 2012 features in different interface.

Feature	Server Core option	Minimal Server Interface	Server with a GUI option	Desktop Experience feature installed
Command prompt	available	available	available	available
Windows PowerShell/Microsoft.NET	available	available	available	available
Server Manager	not available	available	available	available
Microsoft Management Console	not available	available	available	available
Control Panel	not available	not available	available	available
Control Panel applets	not available	some available	available	available
Windows Explorer	not available	not available	available	available
Taskbar	not available	not available	available	available

Notification area	not available	not available	available	available
Internet Explorer	not available	not available	available	available
Built-in help system	not available	not available	available	available
Themes	not available	not available	not available	available
Metro-style Start screen	not available	not available	not available	available
Metro-style apps	not available	not available	not available	available
Windows Media Player	not available	not available	not available	available

1.10: Features on Demand

When feature files are not available on the target server, *Feature on Demand* searches for missing feature files. This is done in three ways.

1. Searching in a location that has been specified by users of the Add Roles and Feature Wizard or DISM installation commands.

2. Examining the configuration of the Group Policy setting by navigating to Computer Configuration\Administrative Templates\System\Specify settings for optional component installation and component repair.

3. Searching Windows Update.

Configuring Features on Demand

Creating a Feature File Store involves three steps.

Step 1: -Create a shared folder on a server on your network.

Step 2: -Verify that the correct permissions are assigned to the feature store. The path should have read permissions for the accounts of the target servers. Note that it is not enough to grant user account access.

Step 3: -Copy the source folder from your Windows Server 2012 installation media to the shared folder that you created in step 1.

Overriding Features on Demand involves Three Steps

Step 1: -Specify an alternate source path as part of the Install-WindowsFeaturecmdlet by adding the –source parameter.

Step 2: -Specify an alternate source path on the Confirm installation options page while you are installing features by using the Add Roles and Features Wizard.

Step 3: -Configure the Group Policy setting, Specify settings for optional component installation and component repair.

Adding a Role or Feature

1. To install a role or feature that has been completely removed, use the following command:

   Install-WindowsFeature<feature_name> -Source wim:d:\sources\install.wim:4

2. Offline VHDs cannot be used as a source for installing roles or features, which have been completely removed.

Removing a Role or Feature

1. To remove a role or feature, use the following command:

   Uninstall-WindowsFeature –Name <feature_name> -ComputerName

   <computer_name> -Remove

1.11: Migrating Roles Overview

Server 2012 role migration is another issue require to take into account because it is great that we can throw in these roles and add and remove them on an as need basis, Server Core or full graphical installation, but often these roles were already being performed on a 2008 or 2003 box. And so as you bring them over to 2012, you want to be ready. In other words, you need to plan each role case as a separate step, but also consider how they integrate? Planning to migrate involves considering questions such as

1. What role is being migrated?

2. Are there multiple roles being consolidated?

3. Are you migrating from x86 or x64?

4. What is the source operating system?

5. Have you evaluated the hardware and supporting requirements?

1.11.1: Migrating Roles from Previous Versions

Role migration from previous versions requires some preparations which have been discussed below. First, you prepare your required environment and then initiate the migration process.

Preparation for Migration Involves

1. Choosing file location.

2. Preparing source server.

3. Preparing destination server.

Migrate the Role

1. Export settings from source server.

2. Configure destination server.

3. Install the role.

4. Migrate settings to destination server.

5. Configure the CA.

1.11.2: Migration Tools

There are numerous of migration tools include Microsoft as well as third party tools. This book focus on two main tools WSMT and Netsh which are explain below. These tools play a very imperative role during the implementation of new server in the existing environment.

WSMT (Windows Server Migration Tool)

WSMT can migrate server roles, features, operating system settings, and shares to either the Server Core or GUI installation of Server 2012.

Five supported migrations using WSMT are listed

1. x86 or x64 versions of Windows Server 2003 with SP2.
2. x86 or x64 version of Windows Server 2003 R2.
3. x86 or x64 versions of Windows Server 2008 (full installation).
4. Windows Server 2008 R2 (full or Server Core installation).
5. Windows Server 2012 (full or Server Core installation).

Netsh

Netsh is a great tool. It is very useful for managing and documenting the settings, and for exporting and importing the settings of a lot of network-based roles such as DHCP, network access policy servers, or remote access servers. Therefore, you use Netsh, to export the NAT and HRA roles, also specifically the network policy service role, and get those out as XML files. Once you exported all of your configuration options that you need using Netsh, you are going to place those exported XML documentation files – those export files – you're going to place them there in that file share which is the middleman between the two servers.

1.12: Server Core environment

After you log on in a server core environment, you are merely with command line. Server core is slim down, remember 4 GB less than a full installation by default. You are going to be presented in server core with just a command line interface, no graphics. However, there are several tools in server core as well and as mentioned before that it is possible to jump into GUI from server core at any time and vice versa.

1.12.1: Tools in server core

Server core depends on powershell and command line interface which offers huge numbers of commands and tools to perform the tasks. Sconfig and RSAT are the very prominent tools in server core environment.

sconfig

sconfig presents a menu-driven interface in the command line Windows. So, it is not graphical, but it is menu driven through which you can pick, choose and get the options done very quickly. Therefore, initial configuration of the box, that is what sconfig is all about – domain, workgroup, computer name, adding a local administrator, managing remote access, defining Windows Update, installing those, defining if your network settings, your IP address, right, all those important elements so you are not just DHCP-based, but you have got the static IP that you want.All of that can be driven through this sconfig interface to save you from having to batch up a bunch of scripts, to do that each time.

These are going to be important steps for the initial configuration. Once this is done, sometimes you can walk away and manage everything using the Remote Server Administration Tools and Server Manager, but initially this is a great tool to have. If you are comfortable using this tool and you like it, one of the great things now in 2012 is that you actually have this same tool available in the full server addition.

RSAT (Remote Server Administration Tools)

Remote management is a great way to work with a Server 2012 environment. With the recommendation and the default behavior of servers to be a command line only Server Core based interface, then the Remote Server Administrative Tools that you can install onto a desktop to remotely manages the server are more important than ever. The *RSAT* for Windows 8 – *Remote Server Administrative Tools* to work on our Windows 8 platform – gives you access to 2012's Server Manager. They can manage multiple servers simultaneously, gives you access to the all the MMC snap-ins, and the command line tools, and the PowerShell cmdlets that are associated with managing a 2012 environment. Besides, Server 2012 enables remote management by default. With it being Server Core by default, with it remote management being enabled by default, using the Remote Server Administrative Tools is definitely going to be a huge advantage. Hence, you may want to lean more heavily on these RSAT tools than you have in the past. To enable Remote Management on a server with a Server 2012 Server Core installation, perform the following steps:

Step 1: -Launch PowerShell by typing powershell at a command prompt.

Step 2: -Type sconfig.

Step 3: -Configure Remote Management.

Step 4: -Enable Remote Management

1.12.2: Convert Between Server Core Installation and GUI Installation

As stated that one of the great features of 2012 is its flexibility, its willingness to go between a Server Core and a full installation. If you either need to add the graphical environment later on, or if you start with a graphical environment, then you want to pair it down the Server Core, piece of cake.

1.13: BPA (Best Practice Analysis)

A graphical installation of Server 2012 supports a very powerful utility to help you analyze whether your system is actually running its roles as effectively or correctly as it should be. In this scenario, a utility of server 2012 called BPA (Best Practice Analysis) is very effective. Some of the features of BPA are briefly refer below.

1. Monitor services through server manager.
2. It scans single or multiple servers or roles simultaneously.
3. The BPA analyzes compliance in several categories and reports reliability, trustworthiness, and effectiveness of a role.

1.14: NIC Teaming

Server 2012 can treat multiple NICs as a single interface. It is also known as *Load-Balancing Failover* or *LBFO*.

1.14.1: NIC Teaming Benefits

1. Improve network performance.
2. Offer continuous network availability.
3. Failover supports if NIC fails.
4. Load balancing for network traffic by combining the bandwidth of NIC adapters.
5. Supports NIC connected to the same or different switches.

1.14.2: Considerations for NIC Teaming

Eight considerations while planning NIC teaming are listed.

1. Team only supports Ethernet NICs.
2. NIC team requires at least one Ethernet NIC.
3. NICs capable of different speeds are permitted on the same team, as long as they all operate on the same speed.
4. Standby NICs of a slower speed can be used to ensure connectivity in case the active NIC fails.
5. Server 2012 supports up to 32 NICs on a team.
6. Failover protection requires at least two Ethernet NICs.
7. NIC teaming permits, but doesn't support more than 2 NICs in a Hyper-V VM.
8. Third-party teaming solutions should never be mixed with Server 2012 NIC teaming.

NOTE: - It is not going to support you teaming wireless 802.11 along with Ethernet. It is got to be all Ethernet, all the time.

1.14.3: Limitations of NIC Teaming

1. Teams only support Ethernet NICs.

2. NIC teams require at least one Ethernet NIC.

3. Server 2012 supports up to 32NICs on a team.

4. NIC teaming permits but does not support more than 2 NICs in a Hyper-V VM.

5. Third party teaming solutions should never be mixed with server 2012 NIC teaming.

Summary

- Window Server 2012 contains new features and capable to perform better than previous versions.

- It has merely two editions stander and datacenter, does not come in enterprise edition.

- Before implementing the server 2012 in production environment, it is required to analyze the existing infrastructure including the hard ware as well as software.

- Up-gradation path from server 2008 & 2008 R2 to server 2012 has been discussed in depth.

- Server 2012 supports two interfaces server core and GUI.

- In terms of flexibility, server 2012 is better than previous one as at any time it can be jumped to GUI interface from server core and vice versa.

- Server core interface offers sconfig tool which is very efficient as it is not required any scripting. It is not graphical, but it is menu driven through which you can pick, choose and get the options done very quickly.

- RSAT is another tool in server core interface to manage remote servers.

- The feature on demand is incredibly a magical feature of server 2012 which supports swapping between both interfaces at any point of time.

- Migration from previous servers 2008 or 2003 has become painless due to the migration tools such as WSMT and Netsh.

- NIC Teaming is the exile for those networks which require huge bandwidth. Server 2012 can treat multiple NICs as a single interface. It is also known as *Load-Balancing Failover* or *LBFO*.

Chapter 2

Storage Management

Objectives

The following objectives are covered in this chapter:

- Hard drives to support server 2012.
- Partition overview with types & features.
- Boot Configuration Data (BCD).
- Hard disk to support virtualization.
- Multitrabyte volumes & Resilient File System.
- Storage management.
- Thin provisioning & Trim storage.

Introduction

Next topic focuses on where you put your data. Now, it is about hard disks which come in different flavors in terms of how you partition them. You start off with a certain amount of size and then break it down into usable space for which you look at the ability to format, initially using either an MBR or GPT, and then within Windows the ability to adopt either a basic or a dynamic disk depending upon whether you are planning on teaming disks together.

Windows Server 2012 has some powerful technology known as storage pools. The ability to use storage pools as well as virtual hard disks allows you to a degree of aliasing – flexibility. You can lie and pretend like you have more storage than you really do until certain time as you actually have acquired the storage you need. This kind of flexibility is going to empower you to be able to do more with less in Server 2012.

2.1: Hard Drive Types

1. Solid state drives.
2. Advanced format drives.
3. Factory –encrypted hard drives.
4. Multiple hard drives.

NOTE: - In multiple hard drives, failover clustering is now supported in standard edition.

2.2: Partitions overview

There are three types of partitions on a disk as follows.

1. **System Partition:** -The system partitions are required for storing system recovery tools, security tools, and storing boot files on multiboot systems.
2. **Recovery partition:** -The recovery partitions are required for storing third-party recovery tools, Windows RE tools, and disk image.

3. **Data partition:** -The data partitions are required for storing user data. These partitions consume most of the space on a drive. Data partitions should be placed on a drive other than the one on which operating system is stored.

NOTE: - Server 2012 supports BIOS, EFI, and UEFI computers. All partitions can be encrypted with BitLocker.

2.2.1: Partition Styles

1. MBR (Master Boot Record).
2. GPT.

Features of MBR

1. BIOS computers must be formatted as MBR.
2. MBR works with BIOS or UEFI. In the case of UEFI, an MBR disk cannot be the primary disk.
3. MBR supports a maximum disk size of 2 TB, making MBR less relevant now that large hard disk drives are becoming more common.
4. MBR tables use 32 bits for storing logical block addresses and size information.
5. Typically, MBR disks can only support up to four standard partitions. We can add more partitions using extended partitions.

Features of GPT

1. In a GPT, the first sector of the disk is reserved for a "protective MBR" such that booting a BIOS-based computer from a GPT disk is supported, but the boot loader ad O/S must both be GPT aware.
2. GPT is adopted from Intel's Unified Extensible Firmware Interface (UEFI) specification.
3. It uses 64 bits for logical block addresses.
4. It supports extremely large hard drives (up to 18 EB).

5. It supports many partitions (as opposed to MBR's four).

6. It disks use redundant partition tables and CRC32 fields for better data structure integrity.

7. GPT tables use version information for forward compatibility.

8. Each GPT partition uses a 36 character Unicode name for user friendly names.

2.2.2: Volume (disk) Types

At this moment, not to be confused with GPT and MBR, we also have the question of working with dynamic or basic disks. Now, where GPT and MBR partitioning are inherently an industry-managed property, so, Intel really developed the UEFI standard that is adopted as a firmware-based platform. It is being used now, after that GPT disks on top to boot from because that is what interacts with that environment. However, when you look at how Windows partitions a disk, you also have that question of whether or not you are defining according to Windows logic which declares that the disk is a basic disk or a dynamic disk. Both have been covered below in brief.

1. **Basic disk:** -Now a basic disk is going to be limited to the partitioning structure that is available on a single disk. So when we're using an MBR-based disk, potentially formatting with NTFS, that's typical, then what we're going to have is initially the ability to create up to four partitions, right. That's what MBR says as you can have up to four partitions.

2. **Dynamics disk:** -Dynamic disks can contain an unlimited number of dynamic volumes that function like the primary partitions used on basic disks. Dynamic disks are able to split or share data among two or more hard disks on a computer.

Dynamic Disk Operations

1. Dynamic disk operations create or delete simple, spanned, striped, mirrored, or RAID-5 volumes.

2. Extend simple and spanned volumes.

3. Remove mirrors from mirrored volumes.

4. Divide mirrored and RAID-5 volumes.

5. Reactivate missing or offline disks.

Types of Dynamic Volumes

1. Simple

2. Spanned

3. Striped

4. Mirrored

5. RAID-5 volumes

2.3: BCD (Boot Configuration Data) Types

One of the tasks you need to be ready to manage is the care and feeding of the boot configuration data store. BCD, the Boot Configuration Data, refers to those files that are used in the process of loading the operating system. You need the BCD to reference how to find that winload.exe that will then get the NTOS kernel and drivers into play, and the fact is there might be more than one place where we have these operating system files. There may be multiple NTOS kernels associated with different versions of the operating system – 2012 and 2008 or maybe two instances of 2012 with some differences. When a multiboot system, especially, need to be ready and aware of how to manage the system by editing the boot configuration data. There are some tools that are associated with boot configuration data management that come with Windows. There may also be third-party tools, however, in-built tools are as below.

1. **BCDedit: -** BCDedit is the first main tool which directly configure, make changes to the individual settings to mirror a particular setting, and then create a copy of it that then could be tweaked, or to create a separate store, even completely, and put entries in that store, and if then you want to export stores from one system into another system. Thus, a lot of flexible things can be done using BCDedit to control the boot process which operating systems are loaded. If I had a multiboot system BCDedit can be used to

remove entries that no longer need to be there anymore. That is the idea behind this tool.

2. **BCDboot: -** The other tool is called BCDboot. It is actually used to define the partitions and the boot environment that you are going to be working with. Therefore, it can be used to set up the actual system partition and to define that Windows partition from a low level. It offers to configure that you want to be able to boot from a VHD. Again, we actually support in Server 2012 the ability to configure the system to boot from VHD without requiring any additional operating system, not requiring that it run with a hypervisor like Hyper-V. However, again to boot into that system, you need to have a reference that knows how to open that up and see it which is driven by the entry that make here in BCDboot.

2.4: Virtual Hard Disk (VHDX)

We are living in a virtual world which is one of the main constructs that you may well work with is a VHD or VHDX file to store your content. The VHD or VHDX file is a virtual hard drive file, and it's initially going to be something that you would associate with working with, say, Hyper-V of virtual world, where you create a virtual operating system. It runs through the hypervisor and through software, taking access to the hardware, and so when it needs to save its data, it can save the individual files within the overall framework of a VHD file. Therefore, it becomes a hard drive on a hard drive. The VHD file has been going around for many generations of Microsoft virtualization. In Windows 2008 R2, you could, in Disk Manager, create a VHD file, but that has been improved to the new VHDX file. In fact, remember this VHD or VHDX file is potentially even bootable.

Virtual Hard Disk (VHDX) Features

1. *V*HDX supports for sizes up to 64 TB.
2. It protects against data corruption by logging updates to VHDX metadata.

3. It has improved performance on large-sector hard disk drives.

4. It has larger block sizes.

5. It has a 4 KB logical sector virtual disk that improves performance for applications that use 4 KB sectors.

6. It has the ability store custom metadata on files.

7. It has smaller file sizes.

8. It can reclaim unused space.

2.5: Multiterabyte Volumes

One of the changes that you get to enjoy in Server 2012 is the ability to really start taking advantage of the multiterabyte disk environment. There are lots of technologies that are associated with working of these larger disks. For example, imagine you have a 2 TB disk that needs to run CHKDSK. It takes a very long time, and that time is spent in the past offline which analysis scan is done in offline state, and therefore, users cannot access files. There may or may not be corruption, but the users cannot work with that environment until all of the analysis and repairs are done, then the entire volume goes online. Thus, administrators would often stick with less than 500 GB-sized partition or volume just to avoid bringing all their data down at once. That was considered a best practice and it was primarily due to the health checks that are associated with CHKDSK. Microsoft's heard a lot of pain, and they are trying to fix the issue in server 2012 by multiterabyte disk environment. The new CHKDSK is there to work with multiterabyte-sized volumes much better.

The process performs all the analysis online. It does not have to lash out everybody off. Now, Server 2012 actively checks the health state of the system volume at anytime, and if there is anything that goes awry with that, they will let the administrator know, to fix the issues.

Features of Multiterabyte Volumes

1. Multiterabyte NTFS volumes can be deployed.

2. Historically, 500 GB was the largest deployment as a security precaution against taking an entire volume offline.

3. CHKDSK now detects corruption while the volume remains available.

4. Analysis phase of CHKDSK has become an online and background task.

5. When CHKDSK finishes its background scan, the administrator is advised that volumes need to be repaired, along with possible solutions.

6. When possible, CHKDSK directly fixes the corruption minimizing offline time.

2.6: Storage Management Overview

Let's talk a little bit about Windows Server 2012 and storage management. Now you have been thinking about disks and formatting and being able to create partitions, build out VHD files and VHDX files to store content. In addition, multiterabyte environments with GPT and suite CHKDSK deals with disks on a single case-by-case basis. Storage management is a topic that really is being embraced by Microsoft at all levels to work with the development of storage as a whole, to be able to support direct and virtualized storage, to be able to work with all sorts of disk arrays and controllers of different types in order to provide access to local- and network-based or SAN-based storage.

Storage Management Features

1. Fully scriptable.

2. Manages remotely.

3. It has WMI-based interface.

4. It can manage remote and virtual storage.

5. It supports Storage Management Initiative – Specification (SMI-S).

6. It is independent of vendor support.

7. It can be managed using PowerShell cmdlts.

8. It provides consistent user experience.

Storage Spaces and Pool

Windows Server 2012 is going to provide some great new functionality for storing our data, using a feature called *storage spaces*. Storage spaces are virtual drives created in storage pools. They can be used the same as a physical hard disk. Moreover, logical storage spaces can be larger than the physical disks which house the pool and also data can be mirrored for redundancy. Moreover, Storage pools are collections of physical storage media that are combined to create a pool of storage.

What are Storage Spaces?

1. The ability to organize physical disks into storage pools, which can be easily expanded by adding disks.
2. Disks can be connected in a variety of ways, through USB, SATA, or Serial Attached SCSI.
3. Storage pools can comprise different size disks using different connections.
4. Storage spaces can also use virtual disks, treating them just like physical disks.
5. Storage spaces have the ability for thin provisioning.
6. Storage spaces are resilient to failure of physical media.

2.7: Resilient File System Overview

ReFS, the *Resilient File System* – if you haven't heard about this yet, definitely want to pay attention. You have the ability in Disk Management when creating volume to format one of your volumes with ReFS. When you use storage spaces, you find ReFS at work as well. ReFS is the new technique that can be used to format particular volumes. Actually, it is a tool that Microsoft has implemented and designed to allow to have exactly what it sounds like – a more resilient file system that is still backwards compatible to NTFS tools that have been around in the past. The underlying engine has changed. Some of the feature sets have changed, but the API remains the same for the tools. Thus, the ReFS technology is designed to help with Fault Tolerance.

Features of Resilient File System

1. Resilient file system stores data so that it is protected from common errors that cause data loss.

2. Metadata in a resilient file system is always protected.

3. User data in it can be protected by file, directory, or volume.

4. It works in conjunction with storage spaces.

5. It maintains compatibility with NTFS and current Windows APIs.

2.8: Thin Provisioning and Trim Storage

Two features that are closely associated with the storage-spaces-based environment are working with thin provisioning and working with trim storage. Let's talk about them separately.

Thin Provisioning

Thin provisioning refers to the fact that you could define a virtual disk as a storage space that may exceed the actual capacity of the disk itself. Imagine when you have a 10 TB storage space and merely 3 TB of actual storage is in-line with the disks presented to it. That is a situation where thinly provisioned the virtual disk. It is not full, not thick, it is thin, its light, its missing it. Furthermore, when you near the edge of the 3 TB limits, start getting notifications to add some more space to this because you are running out of room. At this point, virtual disk have the potential of 10TB or reaching the 3TB that already have. You might want to throw some required data in here, go ahead and attach another disk. So, that is the thin provisioning, just-in-time allocation get the disk when need it, but it is still always been presented as its original size. Do not have to change any shapes, the files would not have to be shuffled or anything like that when we add more storage later on.

Trim Storage

Now the *trim storage* is really the flip side of that. In 10 TB disk, you have 3 TB in space, but you deleted content, and at this point, you are actually only using maybe 500 GBs worth of space.

Now, because of that there is available storage that could be reallocated. Trim storage will notify about enough free room to reallocate some of the associated units that are a part of one particular storage pool and re-associate it with another pool, if you want. So two sides of the same coin, thin provisioning and trim storage. Whether it is just-in-time allocation or reclaiming the unused disk space, this is all part of how that virtual aliased aspect of a storage space based upon storage pools is able to provide with a flexible environment that is suitable for enterprise file storage.

Summary

- Server 2012 supports traditional hard drives and its architecture.
- Partition with MBR and GPT is also considerable in server 2012.
- BCD, the Boot Configuration Data, refers to those files that are used in the process of loading the operating system.
- VHD is the conventional virtual hard drive format of Microsoft, however, VHDX format the extended version of VHD which works for same purpose.
- A novice and efficient volume called multiterabyte volume has been introduced in server 2012 which fills the offline pain for the user during the CHKDISK as it supports online CHKDISK process.
- Storage management is a topic that really is being embraced by Microsoft at all levels to work with the development of storage as a whole, to be able to support direct and virtualized storage, to be able to work with all sorts of disk arrays and controllers of different types in order to provide access to local- and network-based or SAN-based storage.
- ReFS is the new technique that can be used to format particular volumes.
- In thin provisioning, just-enough resource provisioning is used. In trim storage, just-in-time resource provisioning is used and resource is reclaimed after use. The storage space on the server appears as 100 GB, but it is actually 75 GB.

Chapter 3

Shares & Permissions

Objectives

The following objectives are covered in this chapter:

- Overview of file share.
- How file & storage services works in server 2012.
- NTFS permissions & quotas.
- Features of Data De Duplication.
- Offline mode of the clients.
- Role of access based enumeration in file share.
- Volume shadow copy services with new SMB 3.0

Introduction

After the setup of hard drives, a network can be built where data can be shared over the network. It defines user shares and permission in a way where merely legitimate user can get into the resources. In addition, advanced share technologies such as Access-Based Enumeration (hiding what people should not have access to) and data deduplication (the ability that you have to actually eliminate redundant blocks of storage that might be held in multiple shares of the same server). These types of technologies makes share environment more efficient, last longer, and least restructured.

3.1: File Share Overview

The world of file sharing in Server 2012 is actually guided by a newer version of the file sharing protocol that have been using for years. Now, file sharing uses SMB 3.0 instead of older version of SMB. File sharing requires setting of UNC path, NTFS permissions and share permissions. It seems straightforward that allowing access to specific resources that want to make available over the network and it is really painless because the front end of file sharing is not really changed. However, behind the scenes, SMB 3.0 is all about being scalable, resilient, and available for more platforms than it used to be before.

To Ensure Data Access

1. You can use Network File System (NFS) transparent failover,
2. iSCSI transparent failover,
3. Offloaded data transfer,
4. Volume Shadow Copy Service (VSS),
5. Server access to fiber channel storage from guest operating systems is also supported.
6. In addition, SMB multichannel, Hyper-V over SMB, and Mobile Virtual Hard Disks (VHD) are also provided.

3.2: File and Storage Services

If File and Storage Services on Server 2012 have been installed, then as an administrator, need a way to manage those services. And there are different aspects of file services that need to manage overtime. File and storage services include follows.

1. File Services Resource Manager (FSRM).
2. Folder sharing.
3. Distributed File System.
4. Disk quotas.
5. Offline Files.

3.2.1: FSRM

Configuring a file server is a huge responsibility because you are creating an easily accessible environment. And yet, with that same ease of access come greater concerns regarding security and controls for this environment. The range of capacity for the users can be delegated in server 2012 and File Server Resource Manager (FSRM) is one of the tools to perform this task. This tool is available as a feature and through this tool not only can create shares, but also can set up those shares and define the storage limits and storage policies that are associated with the server.

In the shared environment, storage limit is not only based upon the NTFS quota system. It also works for Resilient File System in which NTFS quotas are not available because FSRM can keep tabs of this and provides the reports via e-mails and notifications about this process. In addition, FSRM offers control mechanism rather than set polices for entire volume when users run out of space.

FSRM can define file screen policies and help to determine what types of files are appropriate to save up to the server within certain folders. Furthermore, it can notify if there is something that is being attempting to be uploaded that is not appropriate, or both of these features support an audit mode so you can see what makes sense first, and then according to it you can apply a policy. Through this tool not only shares can be built as well as security such as Access-based Enumeration can be defined. If DFS is installed, it can be linked to a DFS root. Thus, it can be said that several great tools are available within the FSRM-based environment.

Note: You can install FSRM from server manager.

3.3: NTFS Permissions

NTFS permissions work as security controls that can apply on an NTFS or REFS based system. So the NTFS permissions, like the share permissions, are designed with a list of users and groups that are trusted from either a local or a Active Directory system which suggests certain access levels and certain restricted capabilities within that environment.

Permission Types

1. **Explicit:** - Explicit permissions are permissions set by default when a non-child object is created, or when an action is taken to set permissions on objects by parent, child, or non-child.

2. **Inherited:** - Inherited permissions are permissions which are assigned automatically when permission is applied to a parent, for example when permission is applied to a folder, the folder's contents adopt that permission.

Permissions

1. **Full Control:** - The Full Control permission lets users read, write, modify, run executables, change attributes and permissions, and take ownership of folders.

2. **Modify:** -The Modify permission lets users delete, read, write, modify, run executables, and change attributes of files and subfolders.

3. **Read and Execute:** - The Read and Execute permission lets users list contents, load files, and run executables.

4. **List Folder Contents: -** The List Folder Contents permission allows users to list the contents and run executables in folders only.

5. **Read: -** The Read permission lets users list contents and load files.

6. **Write: -** The Write permission lets user's list contents, load files, save files, and change attributes of files.

7. **Special: -** NTFS permissions also include a number of Special permissions, which can be applied to users or groups. These permissions provide the ability to further customize the ways you assign permissions to files and folders.

Combining Share Permissions and NTFS Permissions

1. Share permissions apply only to users accessing an object via the network. NTFS permissions apply to both local and network users.

2. You can use share permissions to manage FAT32 drives and other non-NTFS file systems.

3. Because shared folders rely on both share and NTFS permissions, you can set share permissions to Full Control on a folder and then rely entirely on NTFS permissions to restrict access.

4. The final access permissions that apply to a shared folder are influenced by both the share and NTFS permission entries.

3.3.1: NTFS quotas

The NTFS file system has an interesting attribute that applies to their access control lists. Every file that you make and every folder as well has a property and it called the owner. Now any user who is an owner of a particular file, and you can see this by the way in the Advance Security tab of any NTFS file or folder, any account that is defined as the owner of that file or folder has a backdoor to set permissions. Even if the NTFS permissions say "that user is denied Full Control," that user has the ability to edit the NTFS permissions and gives themselves back whatever permissions they need. Now, the question is why they want to bother doing that, one of those reasons is – Quotas.

Quotas – NTFS quotas are used to control the amount of space that is associated with particular users on the NTFS file system. It is based on owning a file and therefore having that file charged against your NTFS quota. There are two types of quotas.

1. **The hard quota: -** It actually limits your ability to use space.
2. **The soft quota: -** It is essentially an audit trail that will identify how much space that you have set how much space you have available and whether or not you are nearing that amount of space or even exceeding that space.

Often administrators set up a soft quota first and then change it to a hard quota when they are ready to start enforcing rules, once they have gotten the idea, the lay of the land, and what files are out there.

The last node is about threshold values. So a threshold is what allows defining at a percentage of full, so 50%, 75%, 80%, 90% – whatever you want to set because you can set multiple thresholds with values for each one of them.

Two Ways of Quota

There are two ways to manage quotas. The first is through NTFS quotas which can be configured through the properties of drives because it is been formatted with NTFS and there is a **Quota** tab. And on this Quota tab, you can **enable quota management** to limit disk space usage.

NTFS quotas are effective, but it has their key limitation. An NTFS quota has to be applied once for the entire disk, the entire volume. And so if there are seven shares, then a user would have a common set of storage available across all of those shares. NTFS quotas cannot be applied at a directory level and that is a real concern. Also, the new file system, the Resilient File System

(ReFS) introduced in Server 2012, does not support NTFS quotas. Thus, there is need to look at the other way.

Managing quotas through File Server Resource Manager (FSRM) is an effective option. In addition, it gives some great tools to limit space through quotas, also limit file types that are uploaded through file screening, and to really dig deep and observe storage reports.

3.4: Data De Duplication

One of the Server 2012 features that is natively available to a file and storage server is data De-Duplication. Now this feature, when enabled, is designed to provide the benefit of not actually storing the same exact blocks of data more than once, but instead, allowing the system to discover "Hey, I've already got that block over here referenced more and so I don't need to actually store it a second time. The second time I could remove the redundant block of data and just place a link to the original storage location." Similar to associates hard links and NTFS, but an automatic feature that is designed to allow for this linking to take place. Thus, the benefits are associated with reliability, performance, and efficiency.

3.4.1: Data De Duplication Key Features

1. Data de-duplication locates and removes duplications in data without adversely affecting data integrity.
2. The benefits of data de-duplication are reliability, performance, and efficiency.

Typical savings based on file type (Diagram)

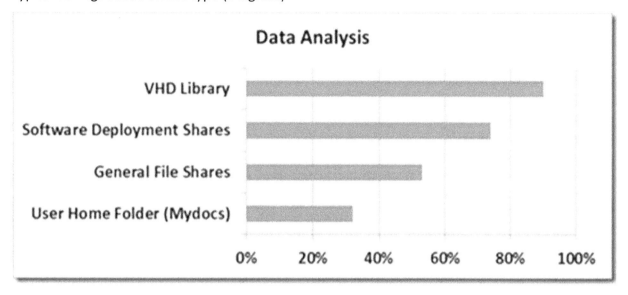

3.4.2: Working of De Duplication

Let's discuses a little bit about how data deduplication does its work. The idea of data deduplication is pretty straightforward, find the redundant bits, and only store them once, and then create links to where those are stored. But the terminology that is associated with this process is to use data deduplication to discover variable-sized chunks. These chunks can be anywhere from 32 to 128K.

3.4.3: Where to Apply

So at this point, you may be wondering – what are the best practices for trying to plan and implement a data deduplication based storage environment? It is a question indeed. Actually, this is a tool for primary data volumes and for data storehouses. It is not going to be there for your system volume or your boot volume, neither is it supported for mapped drives, mapped network drives, or remote mounted drives, anything like that. Generally, data deduplication is intended for the following five points.

1. First, group shares, user folders and offline files.

2. Second, software binaries, updates, and images.

3. Third, VHD file storage for hypervisors.

4. Fourth, volumes those are subject to heavy duplication.

5. Fifth, data that's written infrequently and read frequently.

3.5: Off Line Mode

One of the features of the client operating system that you need to be ready, aware of, and able to take advantage of, and control in the Server 2012 environment is Offline Files, also sometimes known as client-side caching. This is the ability of users to still have access to files even in an offline situation.

User with a laptop connects to a network share and working with a particular set of files that need to reference again at a business meeting in a foreign country where office network is not accessible even through VPN. They could manually create a copy of those files, but, they are going to be flying around to different business meetings at different times and also hop to main office any time. Thus, simply they can tag these files as offline files so that they able to see the most recent copy of it when they online or offline. Server 2012 updates the Offline Files cache at every two hours.

3.6: Access Based Enumeration

Access-based Enumeration – it is a great feature in Server 2012 that allows the ability to simply hide the shares and contents of shares from users who do not have any access to them in the first place. Now remember, you have all sorts of different permissions that can be granted. But if a user is either implicitly or explicitly denied even the ability to read the contents of a share, then Access-based Enumeration is a feature. It says that why shows them the name of the share that they will not be able to work with in any case. Through Access-based Enumeration, users can see only the resources to which they have been assigned permissions.

3.7: Volume Shadow Copy Service

Server 2012 supports the Volume Shadow Copy Service that is been around for several generations and now improves upon it. Now, VSS is associated with the ability to create snapshots of data so as to allow backup applications to back up the snapshot rather than the actual data itself. Because typically applications are working with the data itself and have it locked in such a way that it would not be able to perform a backup of the actual data, but a backup application will have no problem backing up this static snapshot that represents the entirety of the data being selected.

VSS is going to consist of a VSS Requester, like the database application. It says "Please, I like a snapshot. Please help me out." There will be the VSS Writer that is associated with a particular function. So there is a backup writer. There is an exchange writer. There is a Hyper-V writer. There are different writers that are going to work. And then the components – the system and the software elements that are going to be able to have a shadow copy created of them. So, Server 2012 is able to work with NTFS volumes and create shadow copies. Moreover, the Shadow Copy Service in 2012 includes a feature called VSS for SMB 3.0. Remember, SMB 3.0 is the new version of server message block, only available to Server 2012 and clients.

Key Points of VSS

1. With the Volume Shadow Copy Service (VSS), Server 2012 can perform volume backups at regular intervals without interrupting applications that continue to write to a volume.
2. It requires an NTFS Volume.
3. Three components of VSS are listed with examples as follows:

   VSS Requestors: -For example, backup applications.

   VSS Writers: -For example, Microsoft Exchange Server 2010 Writer.

   VSS Providers: -Any components, for example system or software components, that create shadow copies.

Summary

- Microsoft has introduced a new version of SMB with server 2012 that is SMB 3.0. It utilizes the tradition technique with new features to establish file sharing environment.

- File and storage services is the key element for an administrator to manage the files and FSRM, folder sharing, distributed file system, disk quotas and offline files are the key components for it.

- NTFS is not new thing for whom who has been working in windows environment. NTFS permissions and quotas offer the facilities to an administrator to control the users access and space limit.

- Data de-duplication locates and removes duplications in data without adversely affecting data integrity. The benefits of data de-duplication are reliability, performance, and efficiency.

- Recently introduced client operating systems of Microsoft offers a key feature that is offline files, also sometimes called as client-side caching. Server 2012 supports the features via group policy (you will learn about group policy in chapter...).

- Through Access-based Enumeration, users can see only the resources to which they have been assigned permissions.

- VSS is associated with the ability to create snapshots of data so as to allow backup applications to back up the snapshot rather than the actual data itself.

Chapter 4

Storage & Printing

Objectives

The following objectives are covered in this chapter:

- Requirement of iSCSI target server, SMB protocol & ODX.
- Unified & Server manager remote management.
- Role of WinRM.
- Print & Document services with roles.
- Benefits of branch office direct printing, driver isolation, application separation& V4 print driver.
- Print sharing with enhanced points in server 2012.
- Migration of print services.
- Easy print printer driver.
- Function of print pooling, priorities & permissions.

Introduction

The paperless society has not been built yet. So still have printers and a lot of print management in a Server 2012 environment as well that need to know how to administer, setting up that printer so that they can be shared out to the networks to have a central management queue – a place that you configure – that sets the rules for how printing is going to behave. This scenario causes a special options such as printer pooling – being able to assign one logical queue to multiple print devices – or printer priorities, printer scheduling – that allow to set up a set of multiple queues to funnel to the same device, but with different settings to print it different times.

The print driver specifications in Server 2012 have gone through some series upgrades as the ability to use v4 drivers in a more agnostic and flexible way than the way that you worked with drivers classically in previous operating systems. An offline printer management, branch print options are available to print to the right location in a remote environment. Printing options are also encompass permissions and the ability to define who are the right users to be able to administer, to be able to manage documents, or just a print to these print queues define in Server 2012.

4.1: iSCSI Target Server

Another feature that Windows Server 2012 manages natively is the ability to be an iSCSI Target Server. So *iSCSI Target Servers* refer to, in this case, an operating system – Windows Server 2012 – that can make available storage over a TCP/IP network so that remote servers can connect to it and use it as though it was a natively installed on local storage. Thus, this is an economical solution because it is simply using good high-speed Ethernet networks – maybe a GB network switch – to enable storage to be managed through this central component.

In addition, it allows for the older applications to use a Virtual Disk Server Hardware Provider and connect over that iSCSI point of connection. Hence, just head to Server Manager, enable at least the **iSCSI Target Server**, maybe these other features if you want to enable that support.

4.2: Unified Remote Management

One of the new element that is associated with Server 2012 – called *unified remote management for File and Storage Services*. Actually, what it really means is that File Services now enables the ability for administrators to perform various different administrative tasks consistently and universally across multiple servers that are within their environment. Thus, you can create pools of volumes that are on that network, and then manage these storage pools as a single unit. It offers the facility to add and share volumes anywhere within the network. Now, there is no need to manage the individual servers through a whole bunch of separate individual interfaces. It can all be done consistently through a common interface, this one-click process or through scripting, through cmdlet process to work together.

Unified Remote Management of File and Storage Services

1. Unified remote management of File and Storage Services provides a fully scriptable storage management that can be managed remotely.

2. It uses a single, WMI-based interface. It helps in managing a large number of storage systems and virtual local storage, which is also known as Storage Spaces.

3. Storage Management Initiative Specification (SMI-S) allows you to use a single API to manage different storage types.

4. Storage infrastructure should support a valid version of SMI-S or the Storage Management Provider interface.

5. Unified remote management of File and Storage Services provides a number of advantages for enterprise system administrators, and offers comprehensive scriptable management through PowerShell cmdlets.

4.3: SMB (Server Message Block) Protocol

SMB (Server Message Block) Protocol – the protocol used to deliver file shares on Microsoft for years, however, a new upgrade version SMB 3.0 in server 2012 which has some additional features that are designed to support a better delivery, more secure delivery, better high availability and failover technologies, a support for more applications. There are some more performance counters for the application-integrated elements of SMB. For instance, "Let's store my Hyper-V VHD on an SMB share remotely and I can get some good performance with SMB 3.0, or a SQL database could be uploaded to that location." And in some of those locations, may be important to protect the integrity of that data, which can be achieved by enabling SMB encryption.

4.4: Offloaded Data Transfers (ODX)

One of the features now also available in Server 2012 and Windows 8 is called Windows Offloaded Data Transfers or ODX. This ODX feature is best to understand using the concept of just thinking about the way that files get copied from one network storage to another. If you want to copy things from one disk to another, what ends up happening? You end up having to do a buffered read into memory on operating system, and then buffer a write that needs to occur, and then deliver that write instruction over to the remote storage. So if you are copying – whether it is, MB, GB, TB of data – as you are moving that data, it all has to funnel through that host operating system itself. That slows things down. It would be great if there was a way to allow the systems to directly connect to each other, to have these intelligent storage arrays communicate with each other, once you have given them the go command, and say, "Okay I want this file move from point A to point B. You guys take care of it." And that is exactly what ODX does. When you work with a compliant ODX array, you are able to perform these copy operations in such a way where it is offloaded to the storage devices themselves.

ODX and Hyper-V VMs

ODX maximizes network storage services by letting intelligent storage arrays communicate with each other directly. To give Hyper-V VMs access to ODX arrays, there are several possible approaches.

1. You can connect a host or VM to the SMB share of a computer hosted on an ODX-capable array.
2. You can place a VHD on an ODX-capable iSCSI LUN.
3. You can use a VM's iSCSI initiator to manage ODX-capable iSCSI LUNs.
4. You can use a VM's virtual Fiber Channel adapter to manage ODX-capable Fiber Channel LUNs.

Hardware Requirements for Arrays &ODX

Storage arrays using ODX must meet the five hardware requirements, which are as follows.

1. Arrays must be certified to work with Windows Offloaded Data Transfer (ODX).
2. When ODX is used between arrays, the arrays must be from the same hardware vendor.
3. When ODX is used between arrays, the copy manager for the arrays must support cross-storage array ODX.
4. Arrays must be connected using iSCSI, Serial Attached SCSI (SAS), Fiber Channel, or Fiber Channel over Ethernet.
5. Array configurations must be one server with one array, one server with two arrays, two servers with one array, or two servers with two arrays.

4.5: Server Manager Remote Management

When it comes to managing servers in Windows Server 2012, the core tool is Server Manager. Even more than in previous versions of the OS, now, server manager is being the hub around which all the other administrative functions are designed to revolve. Not just for adding roles and features, but as the launch point for tasks related to those specific features, the ability to jump to the management MMCs that are associated with the roles and features. It is all driven through Server Manager. Thus, it is a great tool to be familiar with. Moreover, Server Manager is designed to be able to manage remote servers in a way that is greater than in previous versions.

Using Server Manager to Manage Remote Servers

1. By default, remote management is enabled on servers running Server 2012.
2. Remote servers need to be added to Server Manager's server pool.
3. Remote servers running Windows Server 2008 and Server 2008 R2 can be managed with Windows Management Framework 3.0, .NET Framework 4.0, and performance update KB 2682011.

Configure Server Manager

Support for Server Manager to work remotely is based upon a remote management feature being enabled in Server 2012. And as mentioned, that is enabled by default. Out of the box probably there is no need to do anything. However, if that gets disabled, to re-enable it, all you would need to do is in Server Manager, head to the **Local Server** on the left-hand side and at properties pane that displays all sorts of properties of the server, – its name, the Domain it belongs to. One of the properties that show is remote management. If that says disabled, click that link that opens a nice big dialog box telling "Warning – you are about to enable remote management. That would mean others could manage this server remotely." It is what you have to in mind.

4.6: WinRM

WinRM (the Windows Remote Management) tool is the command line tool that is used to be able to manage the Web Services-Management Protocol. WS management is the technology that is used to, provide management over web services, and it is a overlay on top of SOAP (the Simple Access Object Protocol). In addition, SOAP is an access protocol that is designed to function, using HTTP and HTTPS header structure. When you use WinRM, then actually, you manage the Web Service Listener that is ready to listen to remote request in order to provide functionality for management to happen over a local area network, or a wide area network, or with the Internet, if right ports are enabled.

4.7: Remote Management on Down level OS

In order to enable support for down-level systems to be integrated into the server management using the new Server Manager – the new console – whether managing it from Server 2012 or from the RSAT tools that might have installed on, say Windows 7. Download the RSAT on to desktop, use it to manage all of server environments, to have that centralized management console function, need to enable the down-level clients to be listening for those WinRM requests that are a part of that Server Manager functionality. The components which are required in server 2003, 2003 SP1, 2008 and 2008 R2 have discussed below.

To manage Windows Server 2003 or Server 2003 SP1

1. Windows Management Framework must be installed on Server 2003 computers.
2. Server 2003 computers should be joined to the same domain as the Server 2012 computer.
3. In PowerShell with administrative privileges, type the Enable-psRemoting command and press Enter.

To manage Windows Server 2008 or Server 2008 R2

1. .NET Framework 4, Windows Management Framework 3.0, and Windows performance update KB 2682011 should be installed on Server 2008 computers.
2. Server 2008 computers should be joined to the same domain as the Server 2012 computer.
3. In PowerShell with administrative privileges, type the winrmquickconfig command and press Enter.

4.8: Print and Document Services Overview

The point of enabling Print and Document Services in Server 2012 is to allow the ability to centrally manage those print servers and network printers. These resources that users are needed in order to be able to print out their documents, to be able to take documents and get the physical hard copy of them. But it is also associated with taking scanned documents and delivering them to specific storage locations, or being able to manage fax jobs through the server as well. Five new features of Print and Document Services in Server 2012 have conferred below.

1. Type 4 (v4) Drivers.
2. Branch Office Direct Printing.
3. Print Management Windows PowerShell Module.
4. WSD Secure Printing.
5. OpenXPS Support.

4.9: Roles of Print and Document Services

When install Server 2012's Print and Document Services, then need to figure out about the relevant subservices. The most common one, of course, is being a Print Server. However, all roles have been elucidated as follows.

1. **Print server:** - Administrators can use Print Server to monitor queues and receive notifications if a print queue halts. Using Group Policy, administrators can also migrate print servers and deploy printers. This role includes the Print Management snap-in, which can be used to manage print servers and network printers as well as migrate printers between servers.

2. **Distributed scan server:** - With Distributed Scan Server, users can scan documents using network scanners and send the scanned documents to specific destinations, while administrators can configure network scanners with the Scan Management snap-in.

3. **Internet printing: -** Internet Printing lets users manage their print jobs through a web site, and lets users connect and print to network printers, if they have the Internet Printing Client installed.

4. **LPD (Line Printer Daemon) (Deprecated): -** The Line Printer Daemon (LPD) service (deprecated) allows computers using operating systems that support Line Printer Remote (LPR) printing to print Server 2012 print servers. It is an additional role that can be installed by administrators using UNIX or other systems that support LPR. Note, however, that LPD has been deprecated and may not be supported by future versions of Windows Server.

NOTE: - Print Management console is used to manage print server.

4.10: Branch Office Direct Printing Overview

One of the new features available in Server 2012 is called Branch Office Direct Printing. The idea of this particular service is pretty straightforward. Sometimes users who are printing to print devices in remote offices, but the print server is warehoused in a corporate datacenter on the other side of a WAN link. Now traditionally that would mean that when sending a print job to that printer, the print queue, which is managed there in the main office, has to receive and then send the traffic back to that network printer, which is not a very clean operation. And if for whatever reason that print server or the wide area network link was down, then the user would no longer be able to utilize that particular printer. Thus, the Branch Office Direct Printing scenario, which it can be enabled on a per-printer basis for Windows 2012 Servers working with Windows 8 clients, is going to allow the clients to be able to learn about the printer through the traditional mechanisms. It can be published in Active Directory and can be set up the Print permissions in the same way. But once they have established that connection, then the user will send their print jobs directly to the print device, bypassing the server queue. And, therefore, if the WAN link goes down, if the server goes down, it is not a problem because the user is directly printing there. In addition, at below, five features of Branch Office Direct Printing have also mentioned in brief.

1. Branch Office Direct Printing lets clients print directly to devices.
2. It reduces WAN traffic and server workloads.
3. Clients can print even if the server is down.
4. It is transparent to end users.
5. It can be configured via Print Management console or PowerShell.

NOTE: - It can be enabled on a per-printer basis for Windows 2012 Servers working with Windows 8 clients.

4.11: Driver Isolation

It is not a fun as a print administrator – what's not fun – it is not fun to have a single print driver corrupt your entire print spooler process. It means, managing a print server with 20 print devices that it is managing for the benefit of the clients. They are all sending jobs from time to time. Print driver goes bad, starts acting wonky, and is, just poorly written, needs a patch. But in the meantime, the problem is – it is affecting the way that all of the users are able to use that printer because the spooler service becomes corrupted. And then need to essentially stop the entire spooler service, start a backup again, and get clients connected from the beginning. Most important, it is more difficult to isolate which printer it is having a problem because all the printers went down once that spooler service got corrupted. Thus, to mitigate that problem, there is a tool called *driver isolation*. Driver isolation creates sandboxes for each printer driver when they are set up into an isolated sandbox mode. In addition, if needed, you can set up a shared sandbox that isolates those drivers with other drivers that are set to the shared sandbox mode, but they are not managing with the spooler. Their process memory space is completely separated from the spooler memory space and hence it is a safer way to operate. Driver isolation keeps badly-behaved print drivers from crashing apps. Driver isolation is activated if

1. Enabled by an administrator.
2. Enabled in Group Policy.
3. INF file includes the value Driver Isolation.

4.12: Application Separation

This driver isolation can be go one step further by actually configuring application isolation. And this is probably a good idea for many of us because what we have is, again, that situation. It can develop sometimes where there is a user attempting to print, the print driver crashes, and then the application that they are running ends up crashing as well. That means they may have to kill that particular application and program. If they do that, they may end up discovering that the work that they have done so far has been lost. And, you have to re-enter data, if that is possible. Hence, in order to prevent that type of situation from occurring, a Group Policy configuration setting in Administrative Templates in Printers, similar to the one that we looked at earlier.

4.13: V4 Printer Driver

One of the technologies in Server 2012 Print Management that you need to be aware of is the *v4 printer driver*. The v4 printer driver is like a v3 printer driver, but better. It is faster, leaner, and more flexible than the v3 driver that preceded it. Now they can only be delivered by Windows Update. They are not coming out with the device itself. You are not being asked to install it on demand. Thus, there is kind of a repository – these v4 drivers – that will be built up, that it can install from. But once installed, these drivers are able to set up even with cross-platform, hence they work on both the x86 and x64 platforms. Three features of v4 drivers are listed –

1. Enhanced point and print sharing.
2. No need to install cross-platform drivers.
3. Print Servers no longer driver distribution points.

V4 Driver Design

V4 drivers support print sharing, ARM, Windows Store apps, and simplified driver development. These have been briefly enlightened below.

1. **Print sharing** – V4 printer drivers provide better support for clients (Windows Vista and up) by reducing administrative overhead and the need for multiple architecture drivers.
2. **ARM** – While v3 printer drivers are not supported by Windows running on ARM processors, v4 printer drivers offer print class drivers that run seamlessly.
3. **Windows Store apps** – V4 printer drivers take advantage of common user interface functionality found in the new Windows Store application model, providing a consistent and predictable experience.
4. **Simplified driver development** – V4 driver support all the features found in v3 and XPSDrv driver models and can be easily developed using templates in Visual Studio.

4.13.1: Printer Sharing Overview

Print sharing is the key component of the v4 driver design which has been discussed in this section. So far we looked at using these v4 drivers and the effect that they are going to have. Now, the users are going to have their print drivers brought to them through the installation or through Windows Update. The ability to set up that queue means that the server is not actually handing the drivers out to the client as they have done so in the past. Thus, this changes the model. It changes how much network traffic is occurring. There is an expectation that the client is going to be able to immediately use that printer through that Point and Print environment.

Four features of printer sharing

1. Server provides clients with printer information.
2. Point and Print to send jobs.
3. V3 drivers still usable.
4. Device-specific v4 drivers from OEMs.

Major Changes to the Print Sharing Architecture

Four major changes to the print sharing architecture are listed –

1. V4 drivers.

2. Point and Print compatibility driver.

3. Vista and Windows 7 clients will see V4 drivers as enhanced Point and Print.

4. Clients do not need to connect to server to print.

4.14: Enhanced Point of Print in Server 2012

1. Vista and Windows 7 clients can print to v4 shares without the need for additional software.

2. Windows 8 clients will try to install a v4 driver.

3. Client installation is performed the first time it connects to the server. Print jobs are rendered locally.

4.15: Migrating Print Services to Windows Server 2012

If you are working with an existing print server that is running Server 2003, or Server 2008, 2008 R2, then you may want to migrate that entire collection of print specifications to your 2012-based environment. Through this way there is no need to rebuild all the queues and install all the drivers. You can allow the Migration Wizard process to define those print queues and also lock down the security settings of which users are supposed to access which of our printers. You should configure the sharing settings that are associated with that particular printer.

Printer Migration Wizard migrates

1. Print queues.

2. Security settings for the installed printer.

3. Settings for shared printers.

4. Printer drivers used by the print spooler.

5. The migration from x86 to x64 requires an x64 driver.

How to verify the Migration

1. View event logs.
2. Verify print queues.
3. Print test jobs.

4.16: Easy Print Printer Driver

Another aspect of printing to be aware of is the *Microsoft Easy Print driver*. Now this is a technology. You have seen it for a couple of generations of Windows, but it is closely associated with Terminal Service or now Remote Desktop Service-based environment. The idea is that when a Remote Desktop client or a RemoteApp client is connecting to a session host for their Remote Desktop Services, they may attempt to print something that is an installed driver on the client machine.

In the past, what that would require is that the print server had to have that same driver installed in order for that operation to occur. If it could not find it in its own local driver store, then that printing would fail. Thus, the Microsoft Easy Print provider allows for the client to be able to identify the printer that it is using. After that the Easy Print driver can be used, which provides rich printing, full functionality, all the various different options, duplexing, whatever support is associated with that device. But the process does not involve the server having to go, find, and install those drivers directly on the Terminal Server itself. Instead, the session-based process is able to manage this. Hence, if the Easy Print driver available, generally it is a good thing to use, and it is associated with Remote Desktop Connection clients that are running at least 6.1 and that have the .NET framework installed.

Five Remote Printing Tasks

1. Terminal Services printing for RemoteApp and Remote Desktop sessions.
2. Legacy driver and new printer driver support without needing to install drivers on the terminal server.
3. Printer enumeration by session instead of by user.
4. Rich printing capabilities.
5. Full print driver capabilities.

4.17: Print Pooling

One of the features that any print manager should be well aware of is *printer pooling*. Now this technology says, "Let's set up one logical printer, one printer interface in queue that has multiple ports of exit to physical printers." The benefit there is then that if you have got several physical printers that are in the same location, whether they are TCP/IP printers or local printers that are of the same type process through the same drivers, then you can enable the jobs to essentially load balance between those physical devices.

4.18: Printer Priorities

Another tool that the print server administrator has in Server 2012 is the ability to manage printer priorities. Printer priorities are kind of the opposite of printer pooling. Printer pooling, remember, was one logical interface, one print queue that you see that it points to multiple print devices for load balancing. *Printer priorities,* is going to be two logical printers, two separate queues, one of which will have a different priority value than the other, that both point to the same physical print device.

4.19: Printer Permissions

Printers have something in common with NTFS files and folders, the registry, Active Directory objects, and network shares. What is it? *Access control list* – that contain access control entries that describe the permissions which users and groups will have to this object.

Summary

- Windows server 2012 has ability to work as an iSCSI target server over the TCP/IP network. It provides the storage area as a local storage which is also a Microsoft native feature in servers.

- Unified remote management is a new element which is introduced in server 2012 for file and storage services. It offers administrators to manage the storage services even remotely which saves time and also quite economical for an organization.

- SMB (Server Message Block) protocol is not new in windows environment but server 2012 supports its improved version which is SMB 3.0. It functions same as older one with some new features in terms of better delivery, more secure, high availability, failover technologies and support for more applications.

- One of the features now also available in Server 2012 and Windows 8 is called Windows Offloaded Data Transfers or ODX. This ODX feature is best to understand using the concept of just thinking about the way that files get copied from one network storage to another.

- Server manager in server 2012 supports several new features and managing remote servers as a local server via server manager one of them.

- WinRM (the Windows Remote Management) is a command line tool that is used to be able to manage the Web Services-Management Protocol.

- In order to enable support for down-level systems to be integrated into the server management using the new Server Manager, you need some components on your system such as RSAT on win 7, windows management framework on server 2003, .NET

Framework 4 and windows performance update KB 2682011 should be installed on Server 2008 computers etc.

- Print and document services are the vital features for print administrator as it reduces the work of by creating a centralized print environment with the help of print server.

- There are various other features like branch office direct printing, driver isolation and application separation which pave other ways of printing in case of print server failure.

- A new version of print driver v4 is released with server 2012 print management which is the higher version of v3. Moreover, print sharing is the key component of the v4 print driver.

- Migration of print services from older server to server 2012 is quite common activity for the administrators. Through this way there is no need to rebuild all the queues and install all the drivers.

- For remote users easy print printer driver is a most valuable feature in server 2012. By enabling this feature, a remote user can print the server documents by their local printer. But the process does not involve the server having to go, find, and install those drivers directly on the Terminal Server itself.

- Through print pooling, priorities and permissions, a print administrator manages the users printing activities very efficiently.

Chapter 5

Hyper-V

Objectives

The following objectives are covered in this chapter:

- Virtualization overview & benefits.

- Hypervisors & Hyper-V in server 2012.

- Hyper-V architecture, features, benefits & improved features.

- Hardware & software requirements with planning to install Hyper-V.

- Hyper-V storage & management settings.

- Managing virtual hard drives.

- Differencing disk.

- Hyper-V support for large sector disks.

Introduction

Our next topic is all about virtualization with Hyper-V Server 2012. The Hyper-V process enables to set up hardware, and then put virtual operating systems on top of a host operating system, allowing flexibility to create an environment where multiple operating systems can communicate with each other, with the outside world, all are on physical bugs.

It is not new but server 2012 is equipped with some advance technologies in terms of virtualization. Thus, you can consider Server 2012's ability to deploy out virtualization due to its robust environment to support many virtual machines taking advantage of your hardware, your memory, multiple processors, your physical disks, Fiber Channel, and all sorts of great connections you can make.

5.1: Virtualization Overview

Virtualization is a significant development in IT infrastructure management. Technologies are now readily available and accessible to most organizations. It is suited to most business applications and scenarios.

Why implement virtualization in server 2012? If you have not implemented virtualization yet, the advantages are going to be all about using your resources to the best potential. Nowadays, all organizations are either directly or indirectly utilizing the facilities of cloud computing, virtualization is a core component which makes that happen and it's all about the high availability and the transience, the ability to be mobile from one environment to another. When an operating system is a file that rests upon a hypervisor on a system that can be picked up and moved and dropped on another system with a minimum of time and effort then you end up with a lot of great business continuity.

And there is a technology called *VDI* (*Virtual Desktop Infrastructure*), which means that the users' desktops might actually be a virtual machine, and they are just viewing that virtual machine through one of many interfaces that they used to load that up locally, remotely, and so it is a consistent remote desktop driven access to a virtual machine. Hence, these are some of the many reasons for adopting the virtualization environment and you have not yet, start moving toward a virtualized environment. It is a game changer and worth embracing as well. Next section enlightens some key benefits of virtualization.

5.1.1: Virtualization Benefits

1. Server Consolidation.

    a) These include server consolidation.

    b) Multiple VM's on a single physical machine.

    c) Multiple operating systems on a physical machine.

    d) Reduced TCO for IT infrastructure.

2. Business Continuity and Disaster Recovery.

    a) Cost and complexity is reduced.

    b) Down time is reduced for scheduled and un-scheduled events.

    c) Recovery of virtual machines is simplified.

3. Testing & Development.

    a) First, environments can be built quickly and cost effectively.

    b) Second, easy to mirror the live environment.

    c) And third, changes can be rolled back using snapshots.

NOTE: - The virtualization benefit in heterogeneous system operation support is having multiple operating systems, from different vendors, on a single physical machine.

5.2: Hypervisors

Anytime you start talking about virtualization, you are going to run into a conversation about a hypervisor. So, what is this hypervisor? Imagine you have got two or three virtual machines running on a particular host operating system. Each of those virtual machines is going to be allocated certain number of processors, a certain amount of memory, access to a particular network card.

The *hypervisor* is that piece of software that is going to run underneath all the virtual machines, and in the case of Hyper-V also runs under the host operating system, and doles out the resources to all of these different systems.

Furthermore, hypervisor in Hyper-V 2012 is a thin hypervisor. It does not maintain driver specifications. All the driver information is actually driven through the host server itself which can be observed through the connections that are made between the guest and the parent host operating system. In addition, it is a Type 1 hypervisor, which means it is hardware-dependent for a higher speed operation, so it is going to be using an Intel virtualization chip or an AMD virtualization chip for that support.

Hence, it is an important element to recognize. It is not like the old virtual PC software that Microsoft produced which actually was just software and so your virtual machines were running through software on the host machine, which did not have nearly the performance, speed, and business support that you want and this is why we use a Type 1 hypervisor.

The basic functions of a Hypervisor are

1. To allow multiple operating systems to share a single hardware host.
2. To allocate hosts resources to virtual machines.
3. To ensure that virtual machines do not interrupt each other.

5.3: Hypervisor & Hyper-V in Server 2012

In Server 2012's hypervisor, we see the elements that are needed to create a virtualization based environment. There is the thin hypervisor running at the bottom that is going to provide access to all hardware and the virtual machines. They do not even have their own memory space; they have a virtual memory space that then gets mapped to the actual memory space. There is the hypervisor that provides that quick middleman interface to deliver that. Remember this is a hardware supported function, but it's the mapping table there is driven through the hypervisor itself. In terms of terminology, we have the parent or root partition and child partitions. Essentially thus 2012 host server is going to be the parent partition and then the virtual machines are called the Child Partitions.

When in Hyper-V we want to create a child partition, we go through our properties, we define all the elements, but then we make a hyper call, where our parent partition is going to contact the hypervisor itself and say okay we need to create a construct of resources that is going to be isolated and available for the operating system is running in this partition. And therefore those resources are kept separate from the resources associated with any of the other child partitions or of the parent partition.

Hence, remember the hypervisor itself is pretty dumb. It needs something to provide the instruction set, and it's the APIs that are associated with that parent partition and Hyper-V that give life to that hypervisor and make it really function.

5.4: Hyper-V Architecture

1. The hypervisor provides and maintains separation for the objects running on top of it using partitions.
2. There are two types of partitions, Parent (root) and Child partitions.
3. The virtualization stack runs in the parent partition. Child partitions host the guest OSs.
4. The parent partition hosts Virtualization Service Providers (VSPs), which communicate over the VMBus to handle device access requests from child partitions using Virtualization Service Consumers (VSCs).

In addition, here is essentially a table 5.1 that describes what operating systems are fully supported as enlightened guest operating systems on a Server 2012 Hyper-V system. Now what does that mean to be an enlightened guest? Why are these listed here? If there is an operating system you want to install and it is not listed here, does that mean it's the end of the road? Well no, but what we are seeing is that there are various operating systems that have different editions that can have integration services installed.

Table 5.1: It elucidates the gust OS for the server editions and integration services.

Gust OS	Editions	Integration Services (*denotes that software is not included with server 2012)
Windows Server 2012	All	Included with guest OS
Windows Server 2008 R2 SP1	Standard, Web, Enterprise, Datacenter	Install integration services after guest OS has been installed
Windows Server 2008 R2	Standard, Web, Enterprise, Datacenter	Install integration services after guest OS has been installed (upgrade after installing guest OS)
Windows Server 2008 SP2	Standard, Web, Enterprise, Datacenter (X86 and X64)	Install integration services after guest OS has been installed
Windows Server 2008	Standard, Web, Enterprise, Datacenter (X86 and X64)	Install integration services after guest OS has been installed
Windows Home Server 2011	N/A	Install integration services after guest OS has been installed
Windows Small Business	Essentials, Standard	Install integration services

Server 2011		after guest OS has been installed
Windows Server 2003 R2 SP2	Standard, Web, Enterprise, Datacenter (X86 and X64)	Install integration services after guest OS has been installed
Windows Server 2003 SP2	Standard, Web, Enterprise, Datacenter (X86 and X64)	Install integration services after guest OS has been installed
CentOS 6.0 – 6.2	N/A	Requires Linux Integration Services v3.2. It includes an asterisk sign
Red Hat Enterprise Linux 6.0 – 6.2	N/A	Requires Linux Integration Services v3.2. It includes an asterisk sign
SUSE Linux Enterprise Server 11 SP2	N/A	Included with guest OS
Windows 8	N/A	Included with guest OS
Windows 7 SP1	Ultimate, Enterprise (X86 and X64)	Included with guest OS (upgrade after installing guest OS)
Windows 7	Ultimate, Enterprise (X86 and X64)	Included with guest OS (upgrade after installing guest OS)
Windows Vista SP2	Business, Enterprise, Ultimate	Install integration services after guest OS has been installed
Windows XP SP3	Professional	Install integration services after guest OS has been installed

Windows XP X64 SP2	Professional	Install integration services after guest OS has been installed

5.5: Hyper-V Features and Benefits

Table 5.2: It contains hyper-V features & benefits.

Features	Benefits
Fault Tolerance	Hyper-V is a cluster aware, host clustering will be available for Hyper-V Server 2008 R2
Guest OS Support	Support for simultaneously running different types of operating systems
Ease of Management	SCVMM, Hyper-V management tool
Efficient hardware sharing architecture	Enlightened guests, improved VM performance
Pass-Through disks	For disk I/O intensive applications
Multi-core guest OS support	More processors for guest OSs
VM Migration	Live migration in with Windows Server 2008 R2 Hyper-V and Microsoft Hyper-V Server 2008 R2 providing improved uptime
Dynamic Memory	Memory can be dynamically reallocated between virtual machines in response to the changing workloads
Dynamic Storage	Addition or removal of disks while a VM is running
Virtual Machine Snapshot	Revert to a VM to a previous state, improving backup and recoverability options. Up to 50 per VM
Extensibility	Custom tools, utilities, and enhancements

5.5.1: New or Improved Features of Hyper-V in server 2012

As mentioned, Hyper-V is not a new technology. It is been around for several generations of the Microsoft Server Platform. Thus, what is it that you are going to experience with a Hyper-V in 2012 that makes it any different than what we've seen before? Answer is yes, check below details.

Five new features are listed below

1. Client Hyper-V provides Hyper-V VMs on a desktop OS.
2. Hyper-V for Windows PowerShell.
3. Hyper-V Replica replicates VMs across clusters, storage systems, and datacenters.
4. Storage migration.
5. Virtual Fiber Channel connects VMs to Fiber Channel storage.

Four improved features are also listed below

1. Live migration, migrates VMs on clustered or non-clustered VMs simultaneously.
2. Scalability and resiliency provides improved availability and stability.
3. VHD format allows large, fast virtual drives up to 64 TB.
4. Virtual switch supports network virtualization, multi-tenancy, and additional functionality for monitoring, forwarding and packet filtering.

5.6: Hardware and Software Requirements

Four hardware requirements are listed below

1. An x64-based processor with hardware-assisted virtualization and hardware data execution prevention (DEP) is required. Data execution prevention must be enabled in the BIOS.
2. 4 GB of RAM, which is the additional RAM required for systems running more than 4 VMs, is required.

3. Sufficient HDD space to accommodate the guest OS and VHDs, if necessary, is required.

4. Hardware-assisted virtualization is available for processors that include Intel Virtualization Technology (Intel VT) or AMD's Virtualization (AMD-V) technology.

Three software requirements are also listed below

1. Hyper-V is supported by both GUI installations and Server Core installations.

2. Because Hyper-V is optional for Windows 8 Professional systems, you may need to download and install the required Hyper-V files.

3. Hyper-V supports 32-bit and 64-bit guest operating systems.

5.7: Planning to Install Hyper-V

Four prerequisites to install Hyper-V are listed below.

1. First, a computer running Windows Server 2012.

2. Second, a user account with appropriate administrator rights. To create and manage VMs, you need to be a local Hyper-V administrator or general administrator.

3. Third, sufficient RAM to run the intended number of VMs.

4. And fourth, software for the VM OS.

5.7.1: Drivers and Hardware Compatibility

1. Purchase hardware that has been validated by the Windows Server 2012 Failover Clustering Service.

2. Use Windows Server 2012 digitally signed kernel-mode drivers.

3. Boot start drivers must contain an embedded signature.

4. Microsoft Hyper-V Server shares a common kernel and drivers with Windows Server 2012.

5.8: Hyper-V Storage Considerations

When it comes to storage, there is a couple of things that you need to be thinking about in terms of making sure that you know where content is being stored and what type of content is being stored. You should also know when is it being written to, when is it being read from, these are important things to be aware of. Thus, Hyper-V requires considering the placement of the virtual machine files, the save and snapshot files, as well as the actual virtual hard drive files. Now, the virtual machine files are XML files, you will get to choose where those are located.

Eight Hyper-V storage considerations are listed below

1. Direct Attach Storage (DAS): SATA, eSATA, PATA, SAS, SCSI, USB, Firewire.
2. Storage area networks (SANs): iSCSI, Fiber Channel, SAS.
3. Dynamically expanding virtual hard disks provide storage capacity as needed to store data.
4. Fixed virtual hard disks remain the same size regardless of the amount of data.
5. Modify with the Edit Virtual Hard Disk Wizard.
6. Differencing virtual hard disks provide storage to enable you to make changes to a parent virtual hard disk without altering that disk. The size of the .vhd or .vhdx file for a differencing disk grows as changes are stored to the disk.
7. Virtual hard disks (.VHD and .VHDX).
8. Up to 4 IDE connections per VM.

5.9: Hyper-V Settings Overview

Now, need to understand that build out a particular VM, but there are a lot of shades and details that you can go into for each of those particular subsystems and additional hardware that can supply after the initial installation. Some of key points have been mentioned below.

1. In the Hyper-V, New Virtual Machine Wizard, decide on memory, processor, disk, and networking requirements. Then specify the VM name and location.

2. The Hyper-V machines must use an IDE disk to boot.

3. SCSI can be added after the machine has been created.

4. Additional Hardware may be added later.

5. Additional options may also be chosen later, such as the boot order, amount of memory, and processor assignments.

5.10: Hyper-V Management Settings

Beneath the area where you can manage the hardware itself of the virtual machine, you have a lot of management settings that are available in the properties of a VM. Thus, what are you doing when mucking about in these properties? Well, you are going to be changing the way that the virtual machine responds, administratively. Key components have mentioned below.

1. **Name:** -Edit the name of the VM and make notes.

2. **Integration services:** -Configure enlightened guests.

3. **Snapshot location:** -Specify VHD snapshots storage.

4. **Automatic start action:** -When physical computer starts, do not start VM as it will automatically start if it was running. Always start VM automatically.

5. **Automatic stop action:** -When physical computer shuts down, save the VM state, turn off the VM, and shut down the guest OS.

Hyper-V Management Tools

GUI Tools

1. **Hyper-V Manager** is an MMC snap-in for the management of VMs.

2. **Virtual Machine Connection** provides direct interaction with VM display interfaces.

PowerShell Tools

1. **Hyper-V Module** provides command-line access to all the GUI functionality. It also offers functionality not available through the GUI.

5.11: VHD

When it comes to the storage of data within a Hyper-V system, Server 2012 is going to make available for us virtual hard drives, VHD files, and this is the standard unit of work whether you are talking about laying down the operating system files or storing data files.

Key features

1. A VHD is a single file that acts as a hard drive.
2. It is used to host guest operating systems.
3. A VHD file is of two types, fixed size and dynamically expanding. In fixed size, the size is set when the file is created. In dynamically expanding, the size will grow as needed.

5.12: VHDX

New to Server 2012's Hyper-V is the VHDX file format. Like a VHD file, this VHDX file is there to store the information, the operating system and the data files of a virtual environment. Thus, why would you prefer to use this file format, which is not backwards compatible to say Server 2008 R2? The reasons are:

1. VHDX is new to Windows Server 2012.
2. It provides support for sizes up to 64 TB, protection against data corruption by logging updates to VHDX metadata, and improved performance on large-sector hard disk drives.
3. It has larger block sizes and a 4 KB logical sector virtual disk that improves performance for applications that use 4 KB sectors.
4. It has the ability to store custom metadata on files.
5. It has smaller file sizes and supports reclaiming of unused space.

5.13: Managing Virtual Hard Drives

Now one of the things you want to make sure that you are not confusing between the differences of the chassis, the box of a virtual machine, and the hard drive that you are associating or inserting virtually into that box. Again let's just talk about some of the best practices with regard to storage of VHD and VHDX files.

1. You can create a virtual hard disk, use an existing virtual hard disk, or attach a virtual hard disk later.
2. Three VHD types are dynamically expanding, fixed, or differencing disks.
3. There is an option to copy the contents of a physical hard drive into the newly created virtual hard disk.
4. When choosing to create a differencing disk, you need to specify the location of the parent disk.
5. The maximum VHD size is 2,040 GB, and the maximum VHDX size is 64 TB.
6. Avoid differencing disks on VMs that run server workloads in a production environment.
7. If physical disk space runs out, running VMs with snapshots or virtual hard disks stored on that disk may be paused automatically.

5.14: Differencing Disks

In addition to basic, dynamic and fixed disks, you have the ability to create another type of disk called a *differencing disk* when running through the New Virtual Hard Disk Wizard. So, what is this differencing disk? Why would you use it? Well, "the idea here would be that I could create an existing disk, fixed or dynamic, and in that existing environment, I could, say, configure an operating system, maybe even Sysprep it, and then I could shut it down. Go to the **Properties** of that particular disk and add the attribute of being a Read-Only disk, but the file happens to be a VHD or VHDX file. Then, I go back to the New Virtual Disk Wizard and I say I want to select a differencing disk. And the first thing it's going to ask me is, okay if you're going to create a differencing disk, then you need to tell me not only where do you want to put this new differencing file, but where is the parent file that is associated with this differencing process. Thus, it means that it's going to need to look back to that original operating system VHD file as a root, a source file. And the idea is, this differencing disk will function just like the original disk did, just like that Read-Only baseline disk, only it supports writes where of course the original disk we tagged is Read-Only".

That means that if you had an operating system that has been Sysprepped that then you could boot to the differencing disk in a new virtual machine. And then you could create another operating system with a new differencing disk and point back to that same exact parent Read-Only file, and you would have a new separate differencing disk, a separate operating system, could name it something different, manage it differently, install different systems on it and both systems would run independently, yet for any files that they have that are unchanged or were original to the baseline operating system installation, the both operating systems will point back to that same root differencing environment, the parent disk to the differencing environment.

Hence, the advantage is really all about space and ease of management. It is a quick way to be able to rollout these new operating systems when you have got that as a baseline to work with. Moreover, some key points have been discussed below as well.

1. A Read-Only virtual hard disk known as the parent, and a child virtual hard disk is read-write.
2. Anything written to the disk is only written to the child in the form of a delta between the parent and the differencing disk.
3. Typically, there will be many children to one parent virtual hard disk.
4. Children disks must use the same virtual disk format (VHD or VHDX) as the parent.

NOTE: This is not something associated with Disk Management because this is not a standard type disk. This is a whole virtualization manager controlled process, not something that'd be done natively by host system.

5.15: Hyper-V Support for Large Sector Disks

One more element that is associated with modern server systems is now the ability to work with large sector disks. GPT disks being able to utilize the 4K sector disk environment, and when our VHDs are stored in this environment, you know that VHDX, as a file format, natively integrates and supports this 4K sector size. It can have a logical sector size that matches the physical sector size.

But what about those VHD files? One of the cool things in Server 2012 is that the virtualization stack actually has software to support the 512e or the 4K sector format. So whether it is emulated or not, it can actually provide a low-level support to be able to essentially translate the 512 sector association with a VHD file and the 4K sector associated with the physical host system and get them to match. Hence, Server 2012, for both VHD and VHDX files, can support the large sector sizes. Key features have been discussed below as well.

1. Hard disks have traditionally used 512 byte sectors.
2. Requirements have necessitated larger sector sizes, specifically 4 KB.
3. The 4 KB sector size can cause compatibility issues with software that's designed for the smaller, 512 byte sector format.
4. The 512 byte emulation drives (512e) have been available, offering some of the benefits of 4 KB sector drive while minimizing compatibility issues.
5. The Hyper-V ensures compatibility for newer storage implementations that use the 4 KB sector format.
6. The VHD driver uses 512 byte sectors and doesn't directly support 4 KB sectors, and VHD files couldn't be stored on drives using the 512e or 4 KB sector formats.

7. The Hyper-V lets users store and access VHD files on 4 KB sector drives by transparently providing access and update requests.

Summary

- In IT infrastructure virtualization plays very significant role in terms of economic environment. These days, almost all organizations are preferring virtualization instead of physical environment.

- The hypervisor is that piece of software that is going to run underneath all the virtual machines, and in the case of Hyper-V also runs under the host operating system, and doles out the resources to all of these different systems.

- Hyper-V delivers the life to the hypervisor as it is pretty dump and need set of instructions to work.

- The architecture of Hyper-V comprises with parent and child partitions. In addition, the parent partition hosts Virtualization Service Providers (VSPs), which communicate over the VMBus to handle device access requests from child partitions using Virtualization Service Consumers (VSCs).

- Server 2012 contains some new features of hyper-v, also with improved one.

- Before planning to install hyper-v, need to examine hardware and software compatibility as well.

- Hyper-V requires considering the placement of the virtual machine files, the save and snapshot files, as well as the actual virtual hard drive files. Now, the virtual machine files are XML files, you will get to choose where those are located.

- There are several tools such as hyper-v manager and virtual machine connection in GUI and hyper-v module in powerShell in hyper-v setting through which you can manage the hyper-v.

- VHDX is the new hard disk format in server 2012 to store Hyper-V file as VHD is the ancestor of VHDX. Like a VHD file, this VHDX file is there to store the information, the operating system and the data files of a virtual environment.

- Differencing disk is another type of disk including basic, dynamic and fixed disks in server 2012. This option is available during configuring Hyper-V; it is not a stander disk.
- Virtualization stack in server 2012 has software to support the 512e or 4K sector format which leads VHD and VHDX files to support large sector size.

Chapter 6

Virtualization

Objectives

The following objectives are covered in this chapter:

- Snapshots technique to create, delete & merge in Hyper-V.
- Discusses Different states of virtual machine.
- Use of pass-through disk, IDE, SCSI or iSCSI & SMB 3.0 file share for storage.
- Role of virtual fibre channel.
- Virtual networking overview & its types.
- Determine configuration of host NIC, SR-IOV & virtual switch.
- How to isolate virtual network in VLANs.
- Role of jumbo frames & TCP offloading engine.
- Process of migration & its types of a virtual machine.
- Hyper-V backup techniques & strategies.

Introduction

This chapter continues the discussion of virtualization with Hyper-V in Server 2012 in terms of network management. Server 2012 provides the facility to create multiple switched environments that are isolated from each other, that accessed the outside world, that use VLANs in conjunction perhaps with Cisco switches, and the ability to setup private VLANs that are isolated from each other, even more accessed in the outside world via the same network card, some great technologies that allow for multi-tenancy. You also have the ability as managers to support a rollback feature, an undo feature, because sometimes things go wrong in the virtual environment. However, if you take a snapshot, you have the ability to undo that occurrence by applying that snapshot and undoing that behavior that has occurred in the virtual environment.

Sometimes need to carry out bigger steps when it comes to High Availability, Fault Tolerance, and redundancy, and so you can create an environment with multiple Hyper-V servers which allow you to migrate, have a virtual machine, and float from one server to another with zero downtime potentially for the clients without even requiring a cluster. You can do this over the network now, or could setup a replica server, where a warm standby available for you on a second site. These tools and technologies are going to enable the Hyper-V administrator to support a stable environment for not only the physical servers, but the virtual ones as well.

6.1: Snapshots

In life there can never be enough undo buttons, enough opportunities to fix mistakes, to rollback to a previous point in time when life was good as opposed to the current disaster that you are living in. However, in Hyper-V Server 2012, you are going to be using the tool of a snapshot to allow for a virtualized undo button. What you can do is at any point in time maybe before you apply a patch, before you install a new piece of software, before you install a service pack, before you try something out, you can say let's take a snapshot. And when you do that, it is going to immediately create a backup of the current state of memory. Some key features of snapshots discussed below.

1. Snapshots contain all the state information for a running host VM.

2. They include memory, disk, and hardware configuration information.

3. They are mainly used in test or development environments. Snapshots might also be used in a production environment to create a rollback point when performing an operation, such as patching or installing new software or hardware.

4. New feature in Windows 2012, when a snapshot is deleted, disk space used by the snapshot is returned to the running VM, and it's not necessary to power off the VM to recover this space.

6.1.1: Snapshot Anatomy

1. Snapshots include an AVHD file, which is a differencing disk that references the original VHD and the memory state if the VM is running.

2. When writing to the disk after the snapshot is taken, information is written to the AVHD.

3. The current state of the disk is assembled from the AVHD and the VHD, and performance can be negatively impacted by snapshots.

4. You can have a large number of snapshots for a VM nested and forming a tree-like structure.

6.1.2: Merging Snapshots

One of the tasks that an administrator may need to do is to consolidate the snapshots. When you delete a snapshot that is no longer used, then those files are essentially automatically merged. Any relevant bits are going to be brought forward and so they become a part of the active snapshot or the active VHD file. If you get rid of all the snapshots, then it is going to essentially merge the current state into the original VHD file to make it available to work with, and that is fine in a live environment in a current scenario. Six steps are listed for merging snapshots.

Step 1: Make a note of the order of the files from most recent to oldest.

Step 2: Rename all AVHD extensions to VHD.

Step 3: In Hyper-V Manager, click Edit Disk in the Actions pane.

Step 4: Browse to the most recent VHD in the line, choose reconnect, and then choose the next youngest.

Step 5: Click Edit Disk to open the wizard again, and this time choose Merge.

Step 6: Repeat the process for all VHDs until you are left with just one.

6.1.3: Deleting Snapshots

What about just deleting a snapshot? It seems that's easy, so how easy is it? Process is pretty straightforward. There you are in the Hyper-V Manager and you are going to select a particular snapshot, and then in the Action menu, the right-click menu, you can choose to either Delete Snapshot or Delete Snapshot Subtree. So if you choose to delete a snapshot, of course they will just delete that one. If you choose to delete a snapshot subtree, it deletes that snapshot and everything that comes after it.

6.1.4: Snapshot Storage Location

Where are the snapshot files? This is an important question and the answer of this question is available in two ways. The actual data files that are storing the differencing data relative to a snapshot, once you take a snapshot all new data's are written to that AVHDX file that's a differencing disk, that's going to live right next to the original disk. Because that is the place where you expect to have the disk I/O for the operating system actually be running, and so it gives the best performance. But the other question is what about those restore elements? The restore elements of the VSV and BIN files that are used to save the state of memory and the XML configuration file that stores the state of the virtual machine itself. Where are those stored? Well, those are going to be stored in a Snapshot folder, which is by default going to be inside of the C:\ProgramData\Microsoft\Windows\Hyper-V folder.

6.2: Virtual Machines States

Any virtual machine can be put into one of several states as an administrator who is trying to manage that particular OS from a Central Management Console.

1. A VM can be in a paused or saved state. Actually, pausing a machine is a suspended execution of a VM and keeps all VM states in memory.
2. If the power is lost on the host, the VM's state is lost.
3. Saving a VM's state saves the machine state to disk. This can be used to release memory and CPU resources for other VMs or for the quick restoration of a VM.
4. When restored from the saved state, the VM is returned to the condition that it was in when its state was saved.

6.3: Pass-Through Disk Access

One of the types of disks that administrators can use for a virtual machine is a *pass-through disk*. A pass-through disk references the idea to have a virtual machine access a physical disk. It seems like an exception to the rule and something that may not make sense, means, isn't the whole point of virtualization the fact that you're working with portable, virtual resources? As soon as we connect a virtual machine to a locally accessible hard drive then you are tying that virtual machine to that particular physical box, and generally that is not something you want to do. The advantage of it is going to be that you are going to bypass the translation process that's associated with writing to the file, the VHD or VHDX file, which then causes the subsequent write into the actual operating system host disk. Thus, you have to first write to VHD, and then write to disk right. There is a two-stage process that really makes that happen.

By the way, do not forget that IDE-based disks can support a boot drive that is set up using this pass-through specification. But SCSI-based controllers or SCSI virtual controllers can only accept pass-through disks that are going to be used for data. However, it is not recommended to support booting virtual machines through the virtual SCSI controller, only through the IDE controller.

6.3.1: Configure Pass-Through Disk Access

You need to ensure that there is an offline disk to use a pass-through disk. Five steps to configure pass-through disk access are listed.

Step 1: To take a disk offline, launch Server 2012's Disk Management console snap-in, right-click the disk you want to use as a pass-through disk, and select Offline.

Step 2: In Server Manager, launch the Hyper-V Manager console by clicking the Tools drop-down menu and selecting Hyper-V Manager.

Step 3: In the Hyper-V Manager console, right-click the virtual machine you wish to configure and select Settings.

Step 4: In the Hardware pane, select the drive controller you wish to configure and click the Add button to add an empty drive.

Step 5: Select the new empty drive, select the Physical hard disk radio button, and then select the partition from the drop-down menu.

6.4: IDE, SCSI, or iSCSI

When it comes to the storage connector, the I/O channel, by which our disks are going to gain access to the virtual machine and vice versa. Let's discuss IDE, the SCSI and the iSCSI.

1. IDE drives are the most versatile.
2. The OS must boot from an IDE disk.
3. The legacy guest operating systems can see them. You can only have four IDE disks in one VM.
4. You can have up to four SCSI controllers, each with 64 disks per controller. You cannot boot from SCSI disks, and you must use an enlightened guest OS with Integration Services.

5. The controller used in the host and guest do not have to be the same.

6. You can have a VHD on an IDE controller that connects to a SCSI controller on the guest VM.

7. Performance does not depend on the attachment used on the guest, but on the disk performance on the physical host.

6.5: Storage on SMB 3.0 File Shares

One other thing to keep in mind with regard to storage is the fact that Server 2012 now supports using Hyper-V over SMB 3.0, formally SMB 2.2.Key points are as below.

1. SMB 3.0 supports the ability to configure a VM that can be stored on an SMB file share.

2. Live migrations of running VMs can be performed between non-clustered servers, while VM storage stays on the central SMB share.

3. Administrators can take advantage of VM mobility without the cost associated with clustering hardware.

4. Hyper-V with SMB storage can also use Failover Clustering if High Availability is desired.

6.6: Virtual Fibre Channel

One of the new technologies that are available in Server 2012 is the ability to use virtual Fiber Channel Adapters. In the past only the host system could integrate with a Fiber Channel network. Earlier, if there are a storage area network and a LUN being provided, only the host operating system could take advantage of that directly? Now each virtual machine can add up to four virtual Fiber Channel connectors that can support inside the guest operating system connection to that Fiber-based network.

1. Administrators can connect directly to Fibre Channel storage from within virtual machine guest OSe by making host bus adapter (HBA) ports available to virtual machines.

2. Administrators can use virtualization to optimize tasks and workloads and give them direct access to Fibre Channel storage, and to configure clustering directly from virtual machine guest OSes.

6.6.1: How to Implement a Virtual Fibre Channel Adapter

So, to be able to get the support for the virtual Fiber Channel network that you want make available for the guest operating systems, there are some things you have to be aware of, some constraints you got to put in right there on the front end. Five requirements for implementing a virtual Fibre Channel adapter are listed.

1. You need to have a computer with at least one Fibre Channel host bus adapter (HBA) and a driver that supports virtual Fibre Channel.
2. You also need to have HBA ports that are configured for NPIV.
3. You need to have a SAN, which is NPIV enabled.
4. VMs must be configured for virtual Fibre Channel adapters, using Windows Server 2008, Server 2008 R2, or Server 2012 guest OSes.
5. You need to have logical devices as virtual Fibre Channel doesn't support boot media.

6.7: Virtual Networking Overview

Virtual Networking in Hyper-V is going to be driven by the fact that Hyper-V is going to present to the virtual machines a logical Virtual Switch. This Virtual Switch is going to represent what the network card, both the synthetic and the legacy network cards, have the ability to plug into.

1. Hyper-V virtualizes network hardware sitting between VMs.
2. Virtual Switch Manager replaces Network Manager and allows you to create and configure virtual networks: private, external, and internal.

6.7.1: Virtual Network Types

Three virtual network types are listed – external virtual network, internal virtual network, and private virtual network.

External virtual

1. External virtual network allows systems to connect to each other, the host server, and also to the physical network.
2. VM must bind to a physical adapter in the host server.
3. This type of network is typically used in a production environment, where VMs must be fully accessible.

Internal virtual

1. Internal virtual network allows communication between the VM and the host server.
2. It also allows the VM to communicate with other VMs on the same virtual network.
3. The internal network doesn't bind to a physical adapter in the host server.
4. It is a good fit for testing environments, possibly for installing downloaded updates.

Private virtual network

1. Private virtual network allows systems to communicate with each other, but not with the host server or any other machine on the physical network.
2. It is not bound to a physical adapter.
3. It is suitable for a testing environment where VM are isolated from the physical network and the host server.

Dedicated Adapter

1. Dedicated adapter is the fourth type of virtual network, which is essentially a security provision that creates a subtype of the external network.
2. It assigns a physical adapter on the host server to a VM.

3. The VM connects to the physical network directly via this adapter and it is not available to the host server.

4. The VM cannot communicate directly with the host server, but it can connect to the host server over the network if the host server has another adapter connected to the same network.

5. Dedicated adapter allows for a firewall component to always be in place between a virtual machine and its host. This is an important provision against infection of the host machine.

6.8: Host NIC Configurations

Three host NIC configurations are listed with their descriptions.

1. **Network Adapter:** It requires necessary drivers when Integration Services is installed in the guest OS.

2. **Legacy Network Adapter:** It is used to perform a network installation of a guest OS or when Integration Services won't be installed on the guest OS.

3. **Fibre Channel Adapter:** It accesses Fibre Channel based storage directly from the guest OS. Integration Services are required for this option.

6.9: Single-Root I/O Virtualization (SR-IOV)

One the other tools that is available in server 2012 Hyper-V and need to drill down into the Hardware Acceleration settings on a virtual machine to see it, is the ability to manage *VMQ* (*Virtual Machines Queue*) which again allows for a virtualization of a physical network card to appear as a local network card for all of the systems. Thus, again faster I/O there and Single-root I/O virtualization, another hardware supported component. Brief points have mentioned below.

1. You can assign network adapters directly to VMs, provided the network adapter supports SR-IOV.

2. SR-IOV can optimize network throughput, reduce latency, and reduce the CPU overhead associated with network traffic.

6.10: Virtual Switch

Server 2012's network switches are now an extensible switch with some great improvements for security, multi-tenancy and just a more stable network environment. Five new features of Server 2012 are listed.

1. Server 2012 supports use of extensions by the Network Device Interface Specification (NDIS) filter drivers and Windows Filtering Platform (WFP) callout drivers.
2. It provides tenant isolation.
3. It also provides traffic shaping.
4. It provides added security against malicious VMs.
5. It also provides improved troubleshooting.

Virtual Switch on Server Core

1. When you install the Hyper-V role on a full Windows Server installation, the wizard creates a virtual switch on the first network adapter.
2. When you install on Server Core, this switch creation doesn't take place during the installation. Instead, you have to create the switch after installation and a reboot by using a PowerShell WMI script.
3. To display a list of the options for the vmswitchcmdlet, type the following at the PowerShell prompt and press Enter: get-help *VMSwitch*.

NOTE: - All of the virtual machines require their own unique MAC address and virtual switch manager provides the ability to define the range of MAC addresses that are going to be used. Microsoft basically owns the 00-15-5D prefix for MAC addresses and there is range CEDE00 through CEDEFF that will be assigned for 256 unique MAC addresses.

6.11: VLANs and VLAN Tagging

Virtual Switch supports VLANs as well. You might have the entire Virtual Switch in which network card being assigned a particular VLAN by the physical switch, in this case all the virtual machines behind that host are going to be adopting the same VLAN identifier, no matter what they are communicating with. There are two methods for configuring VLANs, static VLANs and dynamic VLANs.

1. Static VLANs are configured per switch port. The VLAN assigned to a machine will depend on the port it is physically connected to.
2. Dynamic VLANs use the machines NIC to dynamically assign the VLAN using the NIC. They require a NIC that supports VLAN tagging – IEEE 802.1Q.
3. Virtual Switch Manager in Hyper-V allows you to enable VLAN tagging by virtual network, as long as VLAN tagging is supported by the physical NIC.
4. You can also assign VLAN IDs to individual VMs.
5. VLAN tagging is not supported in private networks because they are not bound to a NIC.

6.12: How to Isolate Virtual Networks

1. In hosted solutions, different VMs should never be aware of, or be able to access, others. So, there is a need to create different VLAN IDs.
2. Two drawbacks of VLAN IDs are listed.

    I. 12-bit numbers are limited to 4,094 possible IDs, and the actual number of IDs that can be used is far less, normally 1,000.
    II. Managing multiple VMs, especially in large, datacenter environments, can be a complex task.

3. Hyper-V supports private virtual local area networks (PVLANs), which segment VLANs into multiple broadcast domains.
4. This ensures that each broadcast domain will be isolated from others by assigning multiple IP addresses to VMs.

5. PVLANs can be configured using Port access control lists (ACLs). Each PVLAN uses two VLAN IDs, a primary ID and a secondary ID.

6. PVLANs have three different modes – isolated, promiscuous, and community.

   I. **In isolated mode**, the VM only communicates with promiscuous ports in the PVLAN.

   II. **In promiscuous mode**, the VM communicates with all ports in the VLAN.

   III. **In community mode**, the VM communicates with ports in the same community and all promiscuous ports in the PVLAN.

7. Using PVLANs, you can configure VMs so they can only communicate with the Internet and not with any other VM network traffic by configuring the Hyper-V switch ports of all VMs to share the same PVLAN in isolated mode. The following PowerShell cmdlet isolates the virtual machine EASYNOMAD_WIN8_01 and forces it to use the VLAN IDs 50 and 100:set-vmnetworkadaptervlan –vmname EASYNOMAD_WIN8_01-isolated – primaryvlanid 50 –secondaryvlanid 100.

8. Any subsequent VMs assigned using the same method and ID numbers above will be isolated from each other in the same PVLAN.

6.13: Jumbo Frames and TCP Offloading Engine

There are couple of tools you can take advantage of in Hyper-V that are going to allow for, a kind of a premium experience, when it comes to the performance especially of production machines. Now one of those is the ability to configure jumbo frames. When moving large blocks of data from one location to another or useful when you are dealing with uploading of large files on a regular basis, then the efficient way to deliver that would not be to break it down into 1500 byte frames, but to use larger, up to 9000 byte frames, that can be sent over a network card. Thus, if a network card supports jumbo frames then our virtual network card represented over that can also support jumbo frames. Since Windows Vista you have had the ability to support that within the operating system, only need to enable that though in the properties of the network card, both physically and virtually, in order to take advantage of it.

Three points for jumbo frames are listed

1. A larger than default (1,518 byte) frame can be sent from a network card.

2. Frame sizes up to 9,000 bytes are allowed.

3. Window versions, such as Vista, have supported jumbo frames, but most network adapters have jumbo frames disabled.

Offloaded Data Transfer

1. Offloaded Data Transfer lets you copy large amounts of data between locations in far less time than it might normally take.

2. It offloads the task to host hardware, essentially providing the same performance one would expect in a non-virtual environment.

3. It requires that virtual hard disk files are stored on compatible hardware that's connected to a VM as a virtual SCSI drive, or physical disks that are directly attached to the host.

6.14: Hyper-V Network Virtualization Overview

You want to network your virtual machines and also want that networking to work. Hyper-V in 2012 is all about being able to provide the performance, the integrity, the security, the multi-tenancy that a virtual network environment provides. It starts with just defining your switches that are private, internal, or external, and then builds on that with VLANs, PVLANs, jumbo frames all these different support features and then getting network cards plugged into those particular networks using a hardware acceleration features that might be available depending on the card with which working with. Put it altogether to have a solid network environment to start building on and set up as many virtual machines as you need for a network or for a cloud. Some key points are as below.

1. Network virtualization establishes virtual networks that are independent of the hardware they run on.

2. Virtual networks in Server 2012 are networks comprised of one or more virtual subnets, and the locations of IP subnets are independent of the host environment running virtual environments.

3. Virtual networks can be moved, for example into the cloud, without affecting services and applications.

Network Virtualization Capabilities

Seven key features of Hyper-V virtualization network are listed.

1. Hyper-V virtualization supports network isolation.

2. It provides improved resource allocation.

3. It also provides simplified administration.

4. It supports IP address overlapping.

5. It provides easy movement of workloads.

6. It supports live migration across subnets.

7. It can be configured using PowerShell and Windows Management Instrumentation (WMI). Command-line tools and automated scripts can be created to configure and monitor virtual networks.

6.14.1: Implement Hyper-V Network

There are three ways to implement and configure the network in Hyper-V environment which have been explained below in terms of virtualization 1, 2 and 3.

Hyper-V Network Virtualization 1

In Hyper-V, virtual network adapters are always associated with two IP addresses. In network virtualization, every Customer IP address is mapped to the Provider IP address. VMs send data packets in the Customer IP address space, which is then combined with a provider source and destination address pair. Customer/Provider IP address pairs allow hosts to identify packets by the VM that uses them.

1. **Customer IP address:** It is assigned to the owner of one or more VMs and visible to a VM.
2. **Provider IP address:** It is visible to the physical network, but not available to the VM.

Hyper-V Network Virtualization 2

Hyper-V supports two methods for the virtualization of IP addresses. The two methods are as follows:

1. **Generic Routing Encapsulation (NVGRE):** This is used as a part of tunnel header. The VM's packet is encapsulated within another packet, whose header contains the source and destination IP addresses as well as the virtual subnet ID, which lets hosts identify the source VM. Typically, this is the method that datacenters will use in the deployment of network virtualization.

2. **IP Address Rewrite:** IP address rewrite rewrites source and destination Customer IP Addresses, replacing them with the Provider IP Addresses. When virtual subnet packets reach an endpoint, the Provider IP Addresses are rewritten by the Customer IP Addresses in preparation for delivery to the target VM. IP rewrite is most useful in scenarios where VM workloads utilize 10 Gbps or more of network bandwidth.

Hyper-V Network Virtualization 3

1. In Hyper-V, network virtualization IP address management and policy enforcement are controlled by Windows Network Virtualization (WNV).
2. Every VM network interface is configured using an IPv4 and/or IPv6 address. These Customer IP Addresses are carried by the IP packets sent by VMs and are used by VMs to communicate with each other.
3. To allow management of Hyper-V network virtualization, public APIs are available for datacenter management software, and contain all Hyper-V network virtualization policies.

4. In addition, communication between the Hyper-V network virtualization environment and resources that aren't part of the Hyper-V network virtualization environment may be required if communication between these environments is required.

5. For example, VPN and routing applications require a gateway between them and the Hyper-V virtual network environment. Typically, these gateways can be built on top of Server 2012, or incorporated into load balancers, switches, or network appliances.

6.15: Migrating a Virtual Machine

While VM creation is a one-time activity in the life of a VM, VM migration is an action that might be performed many times. Each VM has a GUID assigned when it is created, and that GUID will follow the VM until it is deleted. There are three basic migration types.

1. **Network migration:** It is the most common migration type and involves transfer from one network host to another.

2. **SAN migration:** It does not require any network transfers. The LUN is removed from a host and presented to a different host using LUN unmasking and masking.

3. **Live migration:** It uses the cluster failover mechanism to fail the VM from one host to another.

6.15.1: Network Migration

1. Network migration is the act of copying a VM across the network.

2. Hyper-V uses Background Intelligence Transfer Service (BITS) for the transfer.

3. It requires System Center Virtual Machine Manager (SCVMM).

4. VMware ESX hosts are supported.

5. Windows Server 2003 and 2008 hosts have to stop or save the VM being transferred. It must remain stopped or saved for the duration of the transfer.

6. Windows Server 2008 R2 hosts can keep the VM running for most of the duration of the transfer. Downtime for a host using Server 2008 R2 is less than a minute in most cases.

7. Windows Server 2012 allows live migration of running VMs, with no downtime during transfer.

6.15.2: SAN (Storage Area Network-based) Migration

1. SAN migration is the process of detaching and reattaching a LUN.
2. It requires System Center Virtual Machine Manager (SCVMM) and one VM per LUN.
3. It uses the Virtual Disk Service (VDS) Hardware Provider or N Port Identification Virtualization (NPIV).
4. The VM is put into a saved state while masking and unmasking takes place.
5. The whole operation should complete in less than a minute.
6. All entities must be able to communicate on the SAN.
7. Most SAN migrations will operate using a Fibre Channel SAN-based connection.

6.15.3: Live Migration

1. Live migration does not disrupt availability.
2. In Server 2008 R2, failover clustering was required. It is not required in Server 2012.
3. Live migration in Hyper-V moves running VMs between physical servers without disrupting VM availability.
4. During migration, the guest OS is unaware that the migration is taking place.
5. Multiple live migrations can be performed simultaneously, making it easier and faster to live migrate VMs. This means that you don't have to set up failover clustering or CSVs, and live migration can occur whether or not the VM storage is local or on an SMB share.
6. Live migration can be extended further to CSV, storage migration and Hyper-V replica. A brief explanation has mentioned below.

Cluster Shared Volumes (CSVs)

1. To minimize downtime, live migration includes a storage option called Cluster Shared Volumes, or CSV.

2. Cluster Shared Volumes (CSV) simplifies Hyper-V virtual machine clusters by allowing multiple VMs to use the same LUN yet fail over independently of one another.

3. CSV can reduce downtime for a migration to less than the typical TCP timeout, meaning that users should not notice any downtime.

4. CSV allows multiple VMs per LUN and dynamic I/O redirection.

5. It is enabled at the cluster level in the Failover Cluster Manager.

6. Cluster Shared Volumes are created as directories under a common root folder.

7. Each VM will be stored in a separate CSV. All Cluster Shared volumes exist under the same namespace, which exists on all cluster nodes.

8. Performance could be an issue with too many machines connected to a single volume, as this configuration is optimized for the fastest live migration with little or no perceived downtime.

Storage Migration

1. In Windows Server 2012, VMs can be stored on SMB file shares and you can perform live migrations on these running VMs.

2. This migration process can be performed between non-clustered servers with Hyper-V installed, and the VM's storage will remain on the SMB share.

3. VM live migrations can also be done between non-clustered servers with Hyper-v installed if local storage is being used for the VM. In this scenario, the VM storage will be mirrored on the destination server first, and then the VM will be migrated, providing uninterrupted service the whole time.

Hyper-V Replica

One of the other technologies that Server 2012 now makes it available is called the *Hyper-V Replica*. The idea of a Hyper-V Replica is that it allows for the replication of our VMs from one storage environment to another, typically a remote site. This is there to allow for a failover scenario.

1. Hyper-V Replica is a storage and workload independent technology that provides regular and asynchronous VM replication over IP networks.

2. This is particularly useful for implementations between remote sites, because if a primary site fails, failover of workloads to secondary sites can occur very quickly with little downtime.

3. In addition, administrators can restore a workload to another point in time as long as it's available in the Recovery History section for the VM.

4. Hyper-V Replica technology doesn't require identical storage and hardware between sites.

6.16: Hyper-V Backup

You need to ensure that you have backed up essentially the content of the host, which is going to be the virtual machines, so Hyper-V host, host of those VHD files, those VHDX files, the XML files, the BIN files, the VSV files all these files that are associated with supporting virtual environment and without those files which do not really have any VMs. Thus, you need to ensure that your host data, which is the VMs, is also being backed up.

1. When considering backup strategies for Hyper-V, you should consider three object types – host OS partition, host data partitions containing VMs, and contents of each hosted VM.

2. That leaves the VM contents, and there are a number of strategies, which can be applied.

Host OS Partition Backup Strategies

1. Servers should be dedicated to running the virtualization role, and this greatly simplifies host OS backup. There's less to backup.

2. Because the host OS partition runs on Windows Server, the standard Windows Server tools – such as Windows Server Backup and third-party backup tools – apply.

3. Other tools for recovery include Last Known Good Configuration, WinPE, WinRE, and Driver Rollback.

Host Data Partition Backup Strategies

1. Data partitions should be part of a shared storage infrastructure with Fault Tolerance and backup.
2. Having the correct infrastructure setup makes the job of backing up these data partitions simpler.

6.16.1: VM Backup Strategies

1. VM backup is a less complex task than you might think, because a VM is simply a set of files on the host OS file system, and therefore can be treated like any other file you'd backup.
2. However, much of the system state information attached to a VM is held in the host's memory, and performing a full backup of the files would require that the VM be shut down.
3. Also, applications within a VM would not be aware that any backup had been performed.
4. Backups can be performed from within a VM to overcome some of these issues. But with a large number of VMs, backup can become difficult to manage.
5. If you are running enlightened guests, another strategy is to use the backup tool to take a Volume Shadow Copy Service (VSS) snapshot of a VM while it is running. The Backup (Volume Snapshot) Integration Service for the guest must be enabled.

6.17: VSS vs. Hyper-V Snapshots

We want to make sure that we are comparing our apples and oranges correctly here. When we talk about *Volume Shadow Copy Snapshots*, *VSS,* we are talking about a backup component that is going to essentially create a temporary image of the files that you are selecting in your backup process and then backing up that image of the files rather than backing up the files themselves. Why? Because we have applications that may have locks in those files and need to be able to continue working with them, and we don't want there to be conflict between the backup process and those applications, or for the application to modify a block of data that is different than the block that you are currently working with and to end up with something its influx that's not quite here or there.

A Hyper-V Snapshot, remember, was an Undo button, the ability to rollback to a previous state. It was a set of files that would be generated when you take a Hyper-V Snapshot that include, essentially, a customized differencing disk and the memory state files that are associated with them when you created the snapshots and even a backup of the configuration files that were taken at the moment of the snapshot. And so Hyper-V Snapshot, and Undo button, VSS Snapshot a temporary set of files used to expedite the backup process of live files. Hence, do not confuse the two taking a test or managing your system.

1. VSS snapshots are not the same as Hyper-V snapshots. Hyper-V snapshots do not create a replica of the data on a VHD, and so are of no use for backup.
2. VSS backups provide a disk image of the complete state of a VM, as well as being application-aware and maintaining consistency.

6.18: Backing Up Within a VM

We have talked about backing up the host, and then talked about backing up the data partitions that hold the VHD and VHDX files. But what if you just want to restore a folder within a particular VM? You do not have that level of granularity with a host level backup. You use some a backup utility from within the virtual machine, whether that's Windows backup or a third-party backup program, you need that capability. Now you can do so using the standard techniques. Follow below steps.

1. Running back up from within a VM is simplified because you can backup to a new volume, then replicate a VHD in a protected network location. Four steps are listed.

Step 1: Create a new dynamically expanding VHD and format it.

Step 2: Create a backup schedule within a VM's OS.

Step 3: Set the new VHD as the target and have the contents replace the contents of the target so there is just one backup set.

Step 4: Use RoboCopy.exe to create a consistent copy of the VHD on the target network location.

2. If a restore is required, you need to mount the VHD and use the original backup tool to perform a restore.

6.19: Windows Server Backup

If you want to perform backups of Windows or the Windows host, the Windows VMs within a Windows guest operating system in Server 2012, then you can also use the *Windows Server Backup*. Now Windows Server Backup is feature that need to install, and then once you have put in this feature, then able to use the management console, the WBAdminmsc and that's available. It is a Storage Manager component that can be a custom console, but again to use this and you have to run both fixed and scheduled backups.

1. Windows Server Backup is the built-in backup tool for Windows Server 2012. It is the replacement for NTBackup in Windows Server versions prior to Windows Server 2008.
2. There are three main interfaces for Windows Server Backup.
   I. The MMC snap-in (WBAdmin.msc) that sits under storage in Server Manager, but can be added to a custom console.
   II. The command line tool wbadmin.exe.
   III. PowerShell cmdlets for use on GUI or Server core installations. If you use them on a remote Server Core installation, you must open relevant firewall ports.

NOTE: - Users must be a member of the local Administrators group or Backup Operators group to use any of these methods.

6.20: Hyper-V Requirements

Once again let's summaries the requirements of the Hyper-V that need to be installed and configured for production environment. Eight Hyper-V requirements are listed.

1. You must have multiple servers capable of running Hyper-V.
2. The servers must use the same CPU brand (Intel or AMD).
3. The servers must be a part of trusted domains.
4. VMS must be configured to use either virtual hard disks or virtual Fibre Channel disks, that is, no physical disks are permitted.
5. It is recommended that a private network is used for live migration bandwidth.
6. In a cluster, Windows Failover Clustering and CSV storage need to be enabled on the cluster.
7. When using shared storage, all required files for a VM must reside on an SMB share.
8. When using shared storage, permissions granting access to Hyper-V servers need to be in place.

Summary

- This chapter is the successor of the previous one and brings the discussion of virtualization with Hyper-V to the next level especially in terms of network management.
- In Hyper-V, there is a tool called snapshot which provide a virtualized undo button. This facility is available at any point of time that create immediate backup of the current state of memory before applying any changes to your production environment.
- An administrator can put virtual machine on several states according to his requirement through central management consol.

- Another type of disk that can be used in virtual machine is pass-through disk. A pass-through disk references the idea to have a virtual machine access a physical disk.

- IDE, SCSI or iSCSI can be the storage options for the virtual machines. In addition, server 2012 supports Hyper-V storage over SMB 3.0 as well.

- Technology is proliferating day by day which leads the support of virtual channel in virtualization. Earlier, merely host system could integrate with fiber channel.

- Virtual networking in Hyper-V depends on the configuration of virtual switch which divides the network in three types (External, Internal and Private virtual network). Moreover, there is another type of network called dedicated adapter which is essentially a security provision that creates a subtype of external network.

- Host NIC can be also configured according to your requirement as virtualization is quite flexible in server 2012.

- To manage the VMQ (Virtual Machine Queue), server 2012 Hyper-V has a tool called SR-IOV.

- Virtual switch in server 2012 virtualization support VLANs that put forward to create and maintain the different VLANs.

- To move or transfer bulky data and to upload a large block of data in server 2012 virtualization environment then there are two tools can be recommended Jumbo Frames and TCP offload Engine.

- Networking in Hyper-V starts with switches that are private, internal, or external, and then builds on that with VLANs, PVLANs.

- Migration of virtual machine is also a part of virtualization. Like host system we perform the migration for virtual machines. Basically, there are three types of migration (Network, SAN and Live migration) that can be performed in server 2012 Hyper-V.

- Similar to normal OS, data and information, there is need to take the backup of the Hyper-V to save the configuration of virtual machine which include VHD, VHDX, XML and BIN files. To perform the accurate back up, need to build a backup strategy before initiating it.

- Always make sure that you are not mixing VSS and Hyper-V snapshots together because both are the different technology and outcomes are also dissimilar.

- Even though you have taken the host back up as well as VM back up, sometime you need some folder and files within the VM. Thus, also need to take the backup within the VM and the tools such as windows backup or third-party backup programs are available for it.

- Windows server backup is a very well-known tool to backup in windows environment and this tool also available in server 2012 to perform the backup process. However, you need to install this feature and once put in this feature then able to use the management console "WBAdminmsc".

Chapter 7

IPv4, CIDR & IPv6

Objectives

The following objectives are covered in this chapter:

- IPv4 functions.
- Differentiation of IP classes.
- Use of public & private IP addresses.
- Role of subnetting, subnet mask & VLSM.
- Need of supernetting& CIDR notation.
- How server 2012 supports router & NAT functionality.
- IPv6 Addressing, features, architecture, representation &types.
- IPv6 & TCP/IP.
- IPv4 & IPv6 interoperability.

Introduction

Our Windows Server 2012 environments require us to define IP addresses on the nodes within our network. That means our clients, our servers, our physical, and our virtual machines, all of that is necessary in order for communication to actually occur. So what you as an administrator really need to know. You need to be able to recognize the heads and tails of an IP address. Now what it means, in a subnet mask means? You are able to understand the idea of subnetting. What is it mean when a subnet mask is different from one environment to the next? How do clients know what's near and what's far? When should they use a router and when should they not?

As we look at networking as a big picture, we see that we moved and are in the process of moving and will continue to move from a IPv4, as a standard, to IPv6, from 32-bit addressing to 128-bit addressing, and from something that is running out of room to something that is scalable to handle multiple planets and not just the earth. Thus, IP discussion in this chapter is going to enable you as an administrator to feel confident when it comes to the later technologies of applying these IP addresses in DHCP and DNS.

7.1: IPv4 Addressing

The IPv4 address – what is this beast? Actually, it is an assignment that is given to a network interface to be able to allow that network interface to know where it lives. Some key points have mentioned below.

1. An IP address is a 32-bit value that uniquely identifies each host.
2. It consists of four octets, each of which is an 8-bit section.
3. An IP address consists of a network portion and host portion.
4. The network portion in an IP address identifies the network the device belongs to.
5. The host portion in an IP address identifies the device on the network.

7.2: Classes

The original specification of IP addresses determined that there would be allocations for different purposes. These allocations determine the types of IP addresses and the size of the IP networks to find by those IP addresses within certain ranges. So these different definitions are called *classes*. Table 7.1 and 7.2 explains different class and purpose of this separation respectively.

Table 7.1: Different classes of IP address.

	0-255	0-255	0-255	0-255	
Class	8 (bits)	16 (bits)	24 (bits)	32 (bits)	Range
Class A	Network	Host	Host	Host	0-127
Class B	Network	Network	Host	Host	128-191
Class C	Network	Network	Network	Host	192-223
Class D	MULTICAST ADDRESS				224-247
Class E	RESERVED				248-255

Table 7.2: Shows purpose of IP address classes and maximum number of hosts.

Class	Purpose	Max. No. of Hosts
Class A	Large Organization	1 67 77 214
Class B	Medium Organization	65 543
Class C	Small Organization	254
Class D	Multicast Addresses	N/A
Class E	Experiments	N/A

7.3: Public and Private IPv4 Address Classes

As the Internet grew in size, it became apparent that there was not going to be enough IP addresses to go around. For every single device it wanted Internet access to be able to have its own unique IP Internet routable address. So a plan was created to allow for the duplication of IP addresses within a local area network, using IP addresses that would never be in use on the Internet. Only behind the boundaries of network address translation that would hide and obscure the duplication. And so network address translation, port address translation, and the adoption of private address ranges have allowed IPv4 to last far beyond the amount of time in which the actual IP ranges themselves would have been depleted. When you have thousands of addresses on all of your systems that are overlapping with each other, obviously those addresses can last longer. The IP private address ranges that are never used on the Internet and are only to be used on private networks and on those private networks are designed to be hidden behind network address translations so that they are never seen even indirectly on the public networks, are specified for the A, B, and C ranges. Table 7.3 and 7.4 contain the range of public and private addresses of class A, B and C respectively.

Table 7.3: Illustrates range of public IP address for global use.

Class	Public Address Range	Routable
Class A	1.0.0.0 to 9.255.255.255, 11.0.0.0 to 126.255.255.255	Yes
Class B	128.0.0.0 to 169.253.255.255, 169.255.0.0 to 172.15.255.255, 172.32.0.0 to 191.255.255.255	Yes
Class C	192.0.0.0 to 192.167.255.255, 192.169.0.0 to 223.255.255.255	Yes

Table 7.4: Depicts range of private IP addresses for private use (within an organization).

Class	Private Address Range	Routable
Class A	10.0.0.0 to 10.255.255.255	Yes
Class B	169.254.0.0 to 169.254.255.255	No
Class B	172.16.0.0 to 172.31.255.255	Yes
Class C	192.168.0.0 to 192.168.255.255	Yes

7.4: Configuring Networks

Network configuration means divide a single large network into multiple smaller networks. You may start off with the big block of addresses, but because you want to have isolated areas within that large network, separated by routing services. That is going to enable you to filter what traffic is able to get from one network to another because you have to cross the boundary of the network. It means, anytime you have a bridge which provides the opportunity to just put down the gates and say no, no one gets across. And that's exactly what you can do with networks as well. Every time you cross from one network to another with the ability to filter and control access.

7.4.1: Subnetting

The benefit of subnetting, of taking one large network and dividing it into multiple networks, involves the security element, but it also involves the performance element. Multiple smaller networks, correctly configured, can benefit in terms of performance relative to one big network where we all just kind of bounce into each other. Even though you work now with switches that isolate traffic for unicast transmissions, your broadcast and multicast transmissions that occur on a network still have to be heard by everyone on that same network. Hence, subnetting isolates the network into smaller chunks.

7.5: Identifying the Network/Subnet

On any network, it's important that a host be able to determine where it lives. It does so by referencing that IP address, that network address that differentiates using the subnet mask, the network, kind of like the street that a particular computer lives on, from its own unique host number, like a house address that you might have for a particular home. By looking at the subnet mask, you can create an intelligent reference that allows you to say, "Ah, I see my IP address, I see how many bits of my IP address are used to reference what network I live on, all the rest would be my unique host bits." Actually, every device in the same network will have the same Network/Subnet ID.

7.5.1: Subnet Masks

Subnet masks are used to identify the network the device belongs to. An IP address means nothing unless you have an accompanying subnet mask because the subnet mask is exactly that. It is a tool to mask out the unique host bits of any IP address and reveal the underlying network ID to hide all of the things that make an IP address unique and to show the street name that that particular house lives on. Thus, you have your default subnet mask. However, when the subnet mask in the IP address comes together it is called a*nding.*

1. Class A addresses have a default subnet mask of 255.0.0.0.
2. Class B addresses have a default subnet mask of 255.255.0.0.
3. Class C addresses have a default subnet mask of 255.255.255.0.

NOTE: - The default subnet mask is also called the classful mask, or natural mask.

7.5.2: Subnetting

There is a need to talk for just a minute about the process and some of the additional jargon that goes around the world of subnetting. Now when you actually kind of dig in and say, what is subnetting going to consist of? How does it actually work? What ends up happening is you've a default network. That default network has a certain subnet mask that defines a certain number of host bits that's indicates essentially how large it is. Answers are below, let's check it out.

1. Subnetting is the process of extending the subnet mask beyond the default mask.
2. The number of bits in the subnet mask beyond the default classful mask represents the number of "borrowed bits".
3. To calculate the number of subnets that a given subnet mask would create first calculate the borrowed bits, which will be the variable S.

   Borrowed bits (S) = (custom subnet mask) – (classful mask)
4. For example, you have the IP address of 172.16.0.0. The default mask is /16. If you applied a custom subnet mask of /20, you would have 4 borrowed bits. 4 borrowed bits = /20 - /16

Now there is couple of more things to be aware of. One of the specifications that come out was something called *Classless Interdomain Routing*. And what it specified is essentially at a high level. The original handoff of IP addresses did not have to be in classful blocks that actually any subnet mask would be potentially assignable for any range. Now you still need to think of your classful specifications when you want to think about what a default subnet mask would be, but it turns out on the Internet these days you never know what the original subnet mask might have been that was handed out by the Internet Assign Numbers Authority to an ISP or to a higher-level organization. Along with that specification of Classless Interdomain Routing or CIDR, that you can at a high level route on the Internet without having to specify a classful default subnet mask, come a shorthand notation called *slash notation*, or *prefix notation*, or sometimes *CIDR notation*. And it's simply a way to shorthand reference our subnet mask. When you use CIDR notation, you use / and a number to designate the number of bits that are 1s in the subnet mask. Thus, based upon the default classes, a class A would be /8, the class B would be /16, the class C will be /24 because that's the number of network bits.

You only have really a few subnet mask to remember, 0, 128, 192, 224, 240, 248, 252, 254, 255, that's it. Those are the only numbers for subnet mask you ever have to worry about. And if you can remember them in that order, increasing by smaller and smaller increments, then it will help you keep track and keep straight the possible subnet mask values. If you were taking an exam, be able to rule-out what's a viable subnet mask and what's not.

7.5.3: VLSM

Another technology to be aware of is called VLSM, *variable length subnet masks*. Now what we kind of started off with is an idea that you're going to have a classful network and then your subnet. And then all of the subnets would be equal parts.

Maybe you start off with a class B, you divide it into 16 smaller networks. Then you realize you know one of these networks does not need to hold certainly 4,000 IP addresses and I actually need to create a smaller set of regions within here that are going to be used may be for wide area networks, remote offices anything like that. Okay, you could take one of those subnets and subnet it further. So, not all subnets of the original class would be the same size.

In this case, let's say you had a /20 and wanted to within that /20, you wanted to divide it further, maybe so that you could guarantee at least 100 hosts in each subnet.

Now remember though you didn't start with class B anymore, you started with /20. So how many networks did you create? If you started with /20 and move forward to /25, then how many bits did you increase? Actually, you went from 20 to 25. So therefore, you have variable lengths subnetted pushing forward 5 to the fifth is 32 subnets of that 1/20 subnet of the original class B network. So that's variable length subnet masking, and it's a tool that you'll utilize in order to create different size networks within your network. This is part for the course and the norm for how you are going to be managing subnets in a 2012 environment. What will be important is ensuring that all of the routers and all of the devices within the same local area network or virtual local area network, if you are using VLANs, are all consistent, that is the key. Make sure everyone is following the same set of rules and then everything works like it is supposed to.

7.6: Supernetting

Supernetting is the process of combining adjacent networks of the same class together. It increases the number of host addresses within a subnet. An example is shown, where the problem is to have 1000 hosts per subnet.

1. In Class A subnet, there are 16777214 hosts. Too many wasted addresses in this subnet.
2. In Class B subnet, there are 65534 hosts. Too many wasted addresses in this subnet.
3. In Class C subnet, there are 254 hosts, too few hosts.

The solution provided for the above mentioned problem is supernetting. There are 254 hosts in the four LANs 192.168.0.0/24, 192.168.1.0/24, 192.168.2.0/24, and 192.168.3.0/24. All the hosts in these four LANs are subnetted to get 1016 hosts.

7.6.1: Subnetting with CIDR

Classless Interdomain Routing – you remember it had that cool notation it was associated with it, right, /24, /22, /26. When we work on the Internet, really, is where CIDR comes into play because you are dealing with the fact that the Internet Assign Numbers Authority can give to a particular ISP or to a large company a block of addresses that was never classful.

1. Supernetting creates more entries in a routing table. It slows routing table lookup.

2. CIDR combines multiple networks into a single network ID. It speeds up routing table lookup.

CIDR Notation

So just in case you missed it somewhere along the way, here is our *CIDR notation*. CIDR notation, or *"slash" notation*, or *prefix notation* is just another way to reference the subnet mask. All it is really saying is – here are the number of network bits in any particular IP address or in the network ID that are used to define the network ID itself. It is great because in documentation trying to look through a subnet mask really is more likely to cause mistakes. What if you forget it 255 or put it in an extra 0 somewhere along the way? Which octet were you in? It is really much more precise to say, there are 22 network bits. Also, when we move to IPv6, which has 128 bits instead of just 32, there is no subnet mask that is created. The notation is different, but one of the things that you will see is things like an IPv6 address and a reference to /48 or /64. They use the management of a slash notation in IPv6 consistently to do the exact same thing to say, in this address here are the numbers of network bits. Thus, be familiar with this concept because really it is great as when you use CIDR notation, it is very easy to say, if you went from /8 to /17, means you just moved forward 9 bits. It is 512 new networks. Hence, it enlightens you what you are moving by, how it's going to be processed in each of these cases. Key points have revealed below.

1. Subnet masks indicate the length of the network portion.
2. Subnet masks must have contiguous 1s.
3. Subnet masks can be written in dotted decimal – that is, 255.0.0.0, or prefix, CIDR, or slash notation, that is, /8.

7.7: Routers

You have spent some time focusing on IP addresses, allocations, subnetting, knowing classes, but remember all of these is based upon the idea that, in addition to the clients with their own network IP addresses, that there will be multi-home devices called *routers* that can provide the handoff from one network to another. Thus, routers are the key to allowing Internet working to function. And there are many types of routers – it is hardware-specific routers made by various different companies such as Cisco and Juniper, you have got software-based routers. *Microsoft Routing and Remote Access* can provide routing functionality and can support receiving packets that were not actually intended for that device, but passing it onto the final destination.

7.7.1: NAT

One of the key functions of many of routers is to provide network address translation. Remember that how public and private IP addresses have been supporting IPv4 long past, the time when all of the IP addresses would have expired if every device that wanted Internet access had a public IP address, was the fact that – in a level of typically a 1,000 to 1 clients in behind, a network address translation (NAT) router can obscure their IP addresses that are actually assigned to the direct machines and instead be commonly using public IP addresses that are available on the Internet. It is done through network address translation typically with port address translation.

Thus, this functionality is absolutely critical to the wave that business has done with IP networks. And Microsoft Routing and Remote Access support the ability to configure not only routing, but network address translation based routing.

7.8: IPv6 Addressing

IPv4 addresses are great, but the fact that there are 32-bit addresses limits them, just like 32-bit processing is limited compared to 64-bit processing. The fact is we need to move to something better. We need an upgrade. That's exactly what IPv6 is all about.

It is not new technology, actually seeing this slowly being implemented into our networks due to its 128-bit scope for IP addresses which offers 340 undecillion addresses to work with. IPv6 is just playing better. It has the ability to address every grain of sand on the earth. It has an improved header structure that is designed to be optimized.

The auto configuration – IPv6 expects there to be an automatic configuration to be able to communicate locally, similar to what you see with APIPA in IPv4 as a failover mechanism, IPv6 implements as a standardized mechanism. An IPv6 has protocols that were invented after the advent of IPv4 incorporated into the underlying structure of IPv6. That is actually a part of the IPv6 structure, which means that then routers can prioritize based upon this information.

Also for security, IPsec, great encryption, authentication, data integrity, and all of that can be provided, but it was an add-on to IPv4 as opposed to actually being an integrated part of the IPv6 stack. So we're going to be adopting IPv6. It's really not a matter of if it's a matter of when. It's being used more and more around the world. Your company may already be a part of the process of working with it. Maybe you participated in IPv6 day and setup Internet support for your sites IPv6 only. But the fact remains, IPv4 is limited and its days are numbered, because just like 32-bit processing compared to 64-bit processing, the needs increase over time. Hence, there is a new technology to be able to support those needs.

7.8.1: IPv6 Features

1. IPv6 has larger address space.
2. It has global reach-ability and flexibility.
3. It supports aggregation, multihoming, auto-configuration, plug-and-play, end-to-end without NAT, and renumbering.
4. IPv4 uses a 32-bit address. IPv6 uses a 128-bit address.
5. Other features of IPv6 include mobility and security. IPv6 are mobile IP RFC-compliant. IPsec is mandatory or native for IPv6. IPsec framework includes IPsec protocol, encryption, authentication, and DH.
6. Choices that are available in IPSec Protocol are ESP, ESP + AH, and AH.
7. Choices that are available in encryption are DES, 3 DES, and AES.

8. Choices that are available in authentication are MD5 and SHA. Choices that are available in DH are DH1, DH2, and DH5.

9. IPv6 has simple header. It has routing efficiency and performance and forwarding rate scalability.

10. It does not support broadcasts and checksums.

11. It has extension headers and flow labels.

7.8.2: IPv6 & TCP/IP stack

1. IPv6 supports IPv4 and IPv6 dual architecture.

2. It shares the same transport and framing layers.

3. IPv6 is a strong host model. It verifies the packets to make sure they are received on the correct interface.

4. Routing compartments in IPv6 isolate traffic for greater security.

5. Windows Filtering Platform, WFP filters local host traffic at all layers of the stack.

6. A new and simple kernel mode programming interface uses the new Winsock Kernel (WSK) instead of the Transport Driver Interface (TDI).

7. It uses new methods of offloading the stack traffic. TCP processing can be offloaded to NDIS network interface adapters and miniport drivers.

7.8.3: IPv6 Architecture

So enter in IPv6, 128 bits you can see that's a lot 1s or 0s, and those are defined with colon-separated chunks. Actually there is not a unique and defined standard term for each of the IPv6 pieces. There have actually been some Internet proposals to come up with a good name for these, but nothing has been ratified. So at this point, you get to call it what you want. They could be called chunks, fields etc. In addition, each hexadecimal number can go between 0 and 15, with F representing 15, D representing 14, so on and so forth. So it means that each one of those, each letter represents half a byte, 4 bits worth of space. Half a byte also is called a *nibble*, so you really got 4 nibbles or a quad nibble or it's sometimes called this a *quibble*, there is even a proposal to call this the *Chazwazza*.

7.8.4: IPv6 Address Representation

Format of an IPv6 address is x:x:x:x:x:x:x:x, where x is a 16-bit hexadecimal field. Hexadecimal A, B, C, D, E, and F are case-sensitive. Leading zeroes in a field are optional. Successive fields of zeroes can be represented as :: only once per address.

Examples of IPv6 addresses:

1. 2031:0000:130F:0000:0000:09C0:876A:130B.

2. FF01:0000:0000:0000:0000:0000:0000:0001.

3. 0000:0000:0000:0000:0000:0000:0000:0001.

4. 0000:0000:0000:0000:0000:0000:0000:0000.

Examples of drop leading zeroes:

1. 2031:0:130F:0:0:9C0:876A:130B.

2. FF01:0:0:0:0:0:0:1.

3. 0:0:0:0:0:0:0:1.

4. 0:0:0:0:0:0:0:0.

Examples of double-colon substitution:

1. 2031:0000:130F::09C0:876A:130B.

2. FF01::0001.

3. ::0001.

4. ::.

Examples of both rules:

1. 2031:0:130F::9C0:876A:130B.

2031::130F::9C0:876A:130B, incorrect.

2. FF01::1.

3. ::1.

4. ::.

7.8.5: IPv6 Address Types

When you communicate over TCP/IPv6, you are going to have some similar things to what you saw on IPv4.IPv6 addresses are of four types:

1. Unicast addresses.

    I.   Link local addresses.

    II.   Site-local addresses.

    III. Global unicast addresses.

2. Multicast addresses.

3. Anycast addresses.

4. Special addresses.

7.9: IPv4 and IPv6 Interoperability

Investing in IPv6 makes sense. We know that this is a technology that's going to be able to support all of the different addresses that we need with the scope, security, and performance benefits that we like. But the world is not all IPv6 yet, and so we're in a time of transition. Still need to support NetBIOS names for resolution, or working with the old days of IPX/SPX and TCP/IP depending on what type of services you need to reach. We're in a time of transition, which means until it's over, we need to be able to support and work with both environments and troubleshoot both environments as we're working with our networks.

Thus, we have a fully dual layered architecture with Windows 2012, Windows 8, Windows 7, and Server 2008 R2. That means we get best performance in both worlds, and we can simply communicate if it's available using the different address technologies as needed.

But sometimes we have to work through intermediate networks that are IPv4 and yet we're using a technology that's based upon IPv6. When that happens, then we'll need to incorporate some sort of mapping technology, some sort of tunneling technology, something that's going to allow the IPv6 environment to traverse the IPv4 environment and then come back to an IPv6 environment. And so we find things like IPv4 compatible addresses and IPv4 mapped addresses that are used to identify IPv4 information in an IPv6 environment or vice-versa. And then we see technologies like ISATAP, another technology that's associated with having a very specific range of addresses that are automatically configured by Server 2012 for each of your IPv4 addresses to be able to communicate directly with each other. There are also technologies like *6to4* and Teredo that are both based upon a type of tunneling. Teredo is actually a Microsoft-developed technology that was built for that very reason.

Summary

- IP address is the heart of the networking environment. Without it cannot event thing about IT world. There are mainly two versions of IP addressing first, IPv4 and second is IPv6.
- There are five classes of IP addressing, however, class A, B and C are the functional class and Class D and E are reserved for especial purpose.
- Public IP are those which are used over internet or in WAN technology. Private IP supports LAN technology and used only in an organization, never use over internet.
- An organization needs to configure its network as a huge network is a complex and hard to manage. Network configuration involves the splitting the large network in small segments.
- Subnetting works as a tool to divide the large network into small. Actually, subnetting isolates the network into smaller chunks.
- Subnetting is the process of extending the subnet mask beyond the default mask.
- Now there is one of more things to be aware of. One of the specifications that come out was something called Classless Interdomain Routing. Along with that specification of Classless Interdomain Routing or CIDR, that you can at a high level route on the Internet without having to specify a classful default subnet mask, come a shorthand notation called slash notation, or prefix notation, or sometimes CIDR notation.

- One more technology need to be aware is called VLSM (Variable Length Subnet Masks). It allows dividing the network in variable size instead of equal size which saves wastage of IP addresses as well.

- Supernetting is the process of combining adjacent networks of the same class together.

- Routers are the key component to build a network. It is hardware-specific as well as software. In server 2012, Microsoft Routing and Remote Access provide the routing functionality logically not physically.

- NAT functionality is also available in server 2012, but, again it is logically only.

- Due to the exhaustion of IPv4, we needed another way to fulfill our internet appetite over the world and IPv6 is that technique. It is better as well as offers large numbers of IP addresses. It supports 128-bit formatting not 32-bit like IPv4.

- Nothing can be changed over the night. In the same way shifting to IPv6 from IPv4 cannot be happened in one sort. Currently, we are in a time of transition, which means until it's over, we need to be able to support and work with both environments and troubleshoot both environments as we are working with our networks.

Chapter 8

DHCP Configuration

Objectives

The following objectives are covered in this chapter:

- Elucidates DHCP services.
- How DHCP assigns IP addresses?
- Methods of IP assignment.
- Fail over techniques of DHCP.
- Planning of DHCP installation & configuration.
- Server topology for DHCP.
- Need of scope splitting technique.
- Why DHCP authorization is need?
- Stored location for DHCP database.
- Function of DHCP on sever core.

Introduction

Configuring correct IP address in a network for the clients can be an arduous and painstaking process when done statically. The technology known as *DHCP*, *Dynamic Host Configuration Protocol*, which is a protocol to configure hosts dynamically. It is a great tool that gets your client setup with an appropriate IP address in the context of their network. This chapter explains building IP scopes in DHCP, give clients the options that they need to appoint them to the router, their default gateway, their DNS server. You will be able to do so in IPv4 or IPv6, in either a stateful or stateless model. And then, when you have got this database of IP addresses that have been handed out to certain clients, tied to their MAC addresses, so you need to make sure you know how to manage that database, how to ensure that it's stable, packed up, and able to be restored later, if necessary.

Moreover, DHCP is a good example of a technology that really operates very well on its own without a lot of maintenance and administrative connections. And so often you want to run it in a high speed, background way, potentially on a Server Core environment. Remember, no graphical interface when you are working in Server Core. So what might you be using if you need to do some quick configuration on that Server Core environment? You guessed it, either NetShell or PowerShell. Thus, these tools are going to be command line-based tools that allow you to import, export, build scopes and do everything you can do from the graphical environment, and allow it to be scriptable and repeatable as well. Hence, if you need to build out a similar environment, maybe in a virtualized location, you will be able to do so quickly.

8.1: DHCP Service

Through DHCP, an administrator is able to set up an address pool, also called the *scope*, which defines the first and last assignable IP addresses to the clients on a lease basis. If the leased IP is not require by the client any more then DHCP also provides the same IP to another client on the network. In addition, along with the IP addresses that are leased out there, an administrator is be able to provide other auxiliary information, like here is your default gateway, your router, here is your DNS server, here is your DNS suffixes, here are your properties for Windows Internet Name Services if using WINS. Moreover, it also allows for reservations, if necessary, static DHCP configuration.

DHCP is powerful enough that you can configure a single DHCP server to support multiple subnets without even needing to necessarily multihome it and plug it into each one of those subnets, if we use a DHCP relay process to, essentially, bounce messages from one subnet into the subnet where the DHCP server is. The DHCP service allows for multicast scope is to be created as well. So if we had a *MADCAP service*, a service that is essentially able to use DHCP to acquire a unique valid multicast address to stream out maybe an image or a video presentation, whatever might be, then multicast addresses could be acquired through DHCP, and then again, given back to DHCP when they're no longer needed. The process of managing a DHCP environment means understanding how it works.

The communication between DHCP client and server is referred as DORA.

- Discover.
- Offer.
- Request.
- Acknowledge

8.2: Assigning IP Addresses

Not unlike games of chance, you can't win if you don't play. And you can't play the IP game in a TCP/IP network until you have a valid, unique, and correctly assigned IP address. So how are these IP addresses going to be set up on a particular system? There are two major processes that work here. One is going to be a manual configuration. An administrator actually going to the system and either through the command line or the graphical interface designated the exact IP specification and properties, such as DNS server sand default gateways, subnet masks, all of the appropriate IP schematics. Second is dynamic process, where we have a service in the network that provides the IP information to our designated system. And so typically we do that through Dynamic Host Configuration Protocol, or DHCP, and that will have a pool of addresses that are available for clients, which may even be other servers to be able to reach out and grab the needed IP addresses to be able to work with the network.

NOTE: - All network devices need a unique IP address and a subnet mask to communicate.

8.2.1: DHCP Assignment Methods

Even in DHCP, there are two process of IP assignment which is mentioned below.

1. In Static Assignment, DHCP assigns a permanent IP address to a client. Static IP addresses are assigned to servers, firewall, and routers.
2. In Dynamic Assignment, DHCP leases an IP address to a client from a scope of addresses. Dynamic IP addresses are assigned to end-user devices.

8.3: Fail Over Techniques

This section discusses the fail over technique for IP assignment. How clients work if a DHCP fails. There are mainly two techniques which are covered in next section.

8.3.1: APIPA

IP addresses as mentioned can be handed out through a manual administrator process or through a server service, such as DHCP, providing the IP addresses to devices that requested over the network. But what happens if a device is set for dynamic, but then the Dynamic Host Configuration Protocol, DHCP server, is off-line or has already handed out all the possible addresses? At that point, a Windows device looking for an IPv4 address is going to failover to APIPA, Automatic Private IP Addressing.

At that point, the DHCP client, with its IP address that itself derives from the class B 169.254 range, will start to function. It'll pick a random number, as we said the last two octets being random based upon that class B prefix at 169.254, and it'll make sure no one else is using that IP address who had agreed to it as ARP, and if someone else has already used that IP address that's in the APIPA range, it'll just try different ones. However, you don't have a default gateway and you don't have a DNS server, you don't have Internet access, you're just kind of stuck in a boat with all your other APIPA buddies that are on the same subnet. So what's the benefit? Actually, you do have physical connectivity and network cards and now you do have a unique IP address within this kind of ad-hoc environment, maybe share files or stream content locally back and forth to each other.

You do have a functioning subnet that might be appropriate for low-level needs. But this isn't really designed for a corporate network to function. This is just a failover technology and most administrators in helpdesk personal are going to recognize, "I see a 169.254 when I do an ipconfig, which means, I need to figure out why this client can't talk to DHCP."

1. APIPA is Automatic Private IP Addressing.
2. A device will assign itself an IP address if a DHCP server is not available in the range 169.254.0.1 to 169.254.255.254.

8.3.2: Alternate Configuration

There is another option too. Instead of APIPA being the failover for a lack of a DHCP server responding, DHCP client services can also failover to an alternate configuration. You might want this when you have an environment where you want to be DHCP-based, maybe in your home network, so that you can access the Internet through your home router. But when you go into the work environment, you need to have a statically assigned IP and maybe reservations are not being configured in your environment. You could set yourself up with the manual IP address and then every time you go home, switch over to DHCP, then every time you go back to work, switch yourself back to your static configuration, but that will be a pain.

With the alternate configuration, you could set up a scenario where assuming you are on a subnet that did not provide DHCP, that's why we didn't use a reservation, then you could have a static assignment, a manual assignment that was locally configured on that box. But if at any time DHCP is available, that is preferred, this also could be used if you knew that you switch back and forth between a statically configured ad-hoc network that you did not want to be on the APIPA range and a DHCP-driven network. This is not used that frequently, in all honesty, but it is nice to have it as an option.

One of the reasons why it is a challenge and something to be aware of is, again, you have to wait for DHCP to time out before you'll attempt to use that alternate configuration. So there is a little bit of a failover time when you bring up the TCP/IP stack because it has to wake up in a DHCP-fewer environment, but it takes time to realize that no DHCP server is responding back.

8.4: DHCP Planning and Configuration

1. During DHCP Planning and Configuration, you need to create and split scopes, add and configure super scopes and multicast scopes, and view and modify scope properties.
2. You also need to activate scopes, multicast scopes, or super scopes, monitor scope leasing activity by reviewing the active leases for each scope, and create reservations for client requiring static address.
3. You can also create DHCP options and required exclusions.

8.4.1: Configuring DHCP Scope

Nine parameters are listed that can be defined for a scope.

1. **Name** – Name, which includes the name of the scope.
2. **Comment** - Comment, which is the optional comment used to describe the scope and its purpose.
3. **IP address range from address** - IP address range from address, which is the start address of the subnet range, address pool.

4. **IP address range to address -** IP address range to address, which is the end address of the subnet range, address pool.

5. **Mask -** Mask, which is the subnet that will be assigned to clients.

6. **Exclusion range start address -** Exclusion range start address (optional) is any IP address within the scope that you do not want the DHCP server to offer or use for DHCP assignment. For example, you can exclude the first 10 addresses exclusion for 192.168.1.0/24 from 192.168.1.60 to 192.168.0.69.

7. **Exclusion range end address -** Exclusion range end address (optional) is as explained earlier.

8. **Lease Duration Unlimited -** Lease Duration Unlimited is the lease period that never expires.

9. **Lease Duration Limited -** Lease Duration Limited is the maximum lease period of the IP address, configured in days, minutes, and seconds.

NOTE: - The ability to manage DHCP using PowerShell is new to Server 2012. We did not have the DHCP module with its cmdlets available previously.

DHCP Scope Reservation

If you have servers, printers, administrative workstations, or laptops that you want to always ensure, use a DHCP-assigned address that remains the same, that remains static over each session that they have, then you want to configure a DHCP reservation. You will find the reservation option available within any of your defined scopes. You build a reservation by saying **New Reservation** from the Action menu. And then it'll prompt you to identify the MAC address, the Media Access Control MAC address of the network card that is going to be requesting a particular IP address. So you'll need to go to the client and acquire that MAC address, ipconfig/all will let you do that. You can bring up the details of a particular network card in the graphical environment. You can use the get MAC command line tool and that'll show that to you as well. Once you've got that MAC address, you'll enter that in the reservation. Thus, you will have a label, the MAC address, you put in the IP address that you want to assign consistently to that particular MAC address. Keep mind that means a reservation would no longer function if you replace the network card on a particular system.

DHCP Exclusions

DHCP exclusions are different than reservations because exclusion is what you never hand out to a client. Now what's reserved for a particular MAC address client, but what is never handed out, so that means manual static configurations that are within an IP range or IP address ranges that are assigned to another DHCP server in a split-scope configuration. So exclusion can be defined after the fact as well when you look at the address pool instead of defining a reservation.

8.5: Server Topology

DHCP is a great service but what about when you have multiple subnets to work with? How does one server support multiple subnets? One method is simply to multihome the server. If you have a server and it has multiple network interfaces, maybe one interface plugged into the 192.168.1.0 network and another one plugged into the 192.168.2.0 subnet, and you create two scopes of 192.168.1.0 scope, maybe with the IP addresses of 192.168.1.50 to 192.168.1.200, and then 192.168.2.0 scope with the IP addresses of 192.168.2.50 through 192.168.2.200. Now when a client sends out its broadcast, it's going to be heard on one of those two interfaces, because the clients either connected to the switch that is on the one side or connected to the switch is on the two sides. And depending on which interface heard that broadcast is going to determine which scope is going to be referenced in order to pull an IP address for the offer to go back to the client. Thus, on multihome, DHCP server works fine. However, sometimes we need to be able to support networks that are simply is not physically possible, or certainly not applicable to be able to set up a multihome device.

8.6: Scope Splitting

DHCP is a powerful service for handing out IP addresses, but what if it goes down? The client boots up, wants to have an IP address, can't get one, somebody is failing over to APIPA, Automatic Private IP Addresses, 169.254 dot something dot something, and you're getting helpdesk calls. So it's a good idea to set up little more high availability, little more resiliency, and Fault Tolerance to the situation by setting up a secondary DHCP server to support any of your subnets.

Actually, DHCP, by default, is an autonomous, self-sustaining, non-replicating process. DHCP servers do not interact to each other. So if you build the scope to support 192.168.2.1 through 192.168.2.200, but what happens if you set up that same scope on another DHCP server? Then our two servers are going to be handing out potentially duplicate IP addresses because they do not know what the other guys handed out.

So what you should look at doing is scope splitting, which says alright, the range of addresses you want to hand out is from, 192.168.2.1 through 192.168.2.200. So how could you set up on the first server an available scope range of 192.168.2.1 to 192.168.2.100 and on the second server from 192.168.2.101 to 192.168.2.200? Hence, scope splitting allows both servers to participate in the DHCP process.

8.7: DHCP Authorization

After the installation of DHCP, there is a post-installation configuration Wizard. And that wizard tells an administrator, your DHCP server – it's great, but it's not going to function, it's not going to respond to any clients until you get it authorized.

Now what does it mean to authorize a DHCP server. Let's associate with the concern about rogue DHCP servers. What if an admin locally installed DHCP, put an IP address on its network card of 10.1.1.1, and then set up a scope for the 10 subnet? But the subnet that they're supposed to be using, that all the clients are using, is the 192.168.1.0 subnet. That's a completely different subnet, those are not interchangeable. You can't just slip on it. And so clients, they don't know who the valid DHCP server is, they accept the offer of whatever gets to their network card first.

When they authorize the server, what it actually does is – puts an entry in Active Directory. And every time the DHCP server service starts, it does an *LDAP* query of its Active Directory environment to authorize. If it's on the list of authorized servers, it'll respond to clients, if it's not authorized, it won't function.

What if you're in a workgroup? If you're in a workgroup, then a DHCP server sends out a DHCP inform broadcast. And if it confined, a DHCP service that is a part of a domain, then it asks that server to send it its LDAP records of who the authorized servers are. So you actually can authorize servers into Active Directory that are not a part of the domain that are in a workgroup, if necessary. But generally speaking, this is designed to be a domain tool.

8.8: DHCP Database and Backup Location

DHCP, as a service, stores it's configuration at a server level, the scopes, and the scope-level configuration, the reservations, the active leases, all these stuff inside of a database. That database is located in the DHCP folder in thesystem32 folder of the systemroot by default.

Additionally, DHCP has this database backed up. This backup occurs automatically every 60 minutes, and we can manually back it up whenever we should so choose. Thus, the backup location is by default just one subfolder below the default location. So systemroot\dhcp\backup is where that's stored. Also, the properties allow designating a different location for the backup directory, so that you can ensure, if the DHCP even drive was to go down, that's okay. Your backup of the DHCP database is still live and could, essentially, restore the service back into another location, if necessary.

Therefore, for best performance and resiliency in terms of disaster recovery, it is best to choose some different locations than the default. Additionally, DHCP is a service that can be managed through a clustered environment and when we have a central cluster-shared storage that is available and then we have multiple servers hosting that one DHCP service, then the actual location will not need to be in the local systemroot directory, but the designation for the database will need to be in that central repository that is accessible by both nodes in that physical cluster.

8.9: DHCP on Server Core

The ability to manage DHCP using PowerShell is new to Server 2012. We did not have the DHCP module with its cmdlets available previously. And we only find these DHCP options once we've installed that DHCP role on the server. So again, these cmdlets are going to enable the ability to build new scopes – v4 scopes, v6 scopes, define server-level options, to manage our reservations, to be able to view connected leases and who is using which IP addresses. Everything you could do from the graphical environment, you can also do from the PowerShell environment. And this tool is designed to be more consistent, more scriptable, and to supplant the process of using netsh to manage DHCP from the command line from now until they hope for something better, really on both Server Core and potentially our graphical installations.

Summary

- DHCP stands for Dynamic Host Configuration Protocol and according to its name it provides the IP to the client systems dynamically over a network.
- The complete communication process between DHCP server and client also referred as DORA (Discover, Offer, Request, and Acknowledgement).
- There are two IP assigning methods in DHCP environment, first dynamic assignment and second Static assignment.

- Even though, DHCP is a very effective and efficient technique in IP assignment, it is possible that sometimes its services get fail. In this situation, APIPA and Alternate Configuration are the two techniques which make DHCP quite robust.

- For the implantation of any project, planning is very crucial. In the same way before installation of DHCP in live network, it is necessary to plan its role and configuration.

- Configuration of DHCP scope is one of the most parts of the planning process. Moreover, DHCP reservation and exclusions are the extended version of the scope configuration which offers some flexibility for an administrator to control network devices.

- There is a shortcoming of DHCP as it cannot support multiple subnets at once. You cannot install spare DHCP servers in a subnet as a backup server.

- Scope splitting is a technique in the DHCP which provides redundancy in a network. You can install two DHCP servers by splitting the scope of IP addressing for the client systems.

- It is a very interesting thing about the DHCP services that if your DHCP server is not a authorized server from Active Directory then it could not offer IPs to the clients. To authorize it an administrator has to complete post-configuration wizard after the installation of DHCP.

- Like other software in Microsoft environment there is a default folder where all the configuration of the DHCP store in the form of database which is located in the DHCP folder in the system32 folder of the systemroot by default.

- Server core also supports DHCP functionality with cmdlets tools like netsh. However, DHCP can be controlled by the PoowerShell that is a new feature in server 2012.

Chapter 9

DNS

Objectives

The following objectives are covered in this chapter:

- DNS overview with its elements.
- Process of DNS in a network.
- Role of DNS in AD DS.
- How referrals and quires work together in a DNS process.
- DNS components.
- DNS records.
- New features of DNS in server 2012.

Introduction

When we look at DNS, domain name services, in a Windows Server 2012 R2 environment, it is important to understand we are looking at both a server configuration as well as a client configuration that work together. Remember, DNS is a service that allows computers to be able to essentially establish a connection to a name that is associated with an IP address by looking up the IP address via the name through almost a centralized phone book of DNS Services. Thus, we can then send and receive information over the network, Internet, and establish connections for all the various different types of services that we generally use.

This chapter elucidates about setting up DNS server role, building that phone book, and then integrating primary zones into a DNS being able to set up forwarders and route hints to be able to establish connections to other DNS servers. In addition, enlightens ability to work with the DNS cache, which is also used in troubleshooting and in maintenance.

9.1: DNS Overview

DNS, the domain name system, is going to be when it's working correctly, a wonderful tool that is going to enable your clients to use, easy to read, easy to type names as a way to reference the services that they would like to be able to reach out and use over the network, like the file services, the domain services, databases. Thus, you need to ensure that you have a stable DNS environment to be able to locate and connect to the various IP resources in your network. But you also need to be able to work with the Internet resources, the web services, and all the components that are going to download from the outside world.

We have got thousands and thousands and thousands of DNS servers on the Internet, and that are maintained within the walls in certain companies. And these DNS servers are there to provide knowledge not of everything, but of just their little bailiwick, their little area of expertise. But they have the ability to go find the authoritative server that is in charge of other things. That's because it is the entire DNS infrastructure is arranged in this top-down hierarchy.

Within the walls of your company, you build out your own DNS server that has all of the information of Active Directory domain. However, what about if Active Directory domain has multiple branches to its tree, multiple namespaces to consider? You will have to establish something similar to what we had on the Internet – but just for your own internal space – and then provide connection points to the external world as well.

Elements of DNS

1. **The DNS namespace:** - The DNS comprises of a tree-structured namespace with identical domain in each tree branch. The information like host name, IP addresses etc. are associated with each domain as a resource records. From any particular domain, query operations fetch explicit resource records.

2. **Name servers:** - A DNS server upholds the authoritative information about one or more specific domains in the domain tree structure which run as an application on server. This allows a DNS server to explore the information about any domain in the tree.

3. **Resolvers:** - A resolver works on client side which makes DNS queries for fulfillment of DNS server process. Minimum one DNS server is accessible by a resolver directly that helps it to process referrals to direct its queries to other servers if necessary.

9.2: DNS Process in Network

Let's talk a little bit about the DNS process – what's really going on. A client is recognizing that someone typed in a name. But in order to connect to a service, it's going to have to utilize an IP address. It's going to look to its cache and see if it's already looked up information before. And if it hasn't, then it'll contact its DNS server. The DNS server is going to say, "Am I in charge of that name that you're trying to look up?" And if the answer is yes, then the response goes back immediately – here's the IP address you want. But if the answer is no, it's not in charge of that namespace. Then each DNS server is programmed with the information to contact the Internet root servers. So to contact that root server and say, "Root server, I'm looking for this address," and the root server will then typically tell that particular server that made this request, "I'm sorry, what you're looking for? I am in charge of it. But I delegated authority to this other server like for example, a .com server."

Thus, server can contact a .com server on the client's behalf. It'll contact the com server and say, "Com server, here is what I'm looking for." And "Can you help me?" The com server says, "I know what you're looking for, and I'm authoritative for that because it does end in .com, but I delegated authority to this second-level domain server." So it gives the second-level DNS server information to my DNS server. My DNS server then contacts that second-level DNS server and says, "Hey, can you give me the IP address of this name?" And since that second-level DNS server is authoritative for that particular name, it will then provide the actual IP address back to my DNS server. My DNS server now has this information. It'll cache it, and give it to the client. And then as a client, I will be able to directly connect to that actual resource, the web server – whatever it is – because I have got the IP address, so now I can establish a connection.

9.3: DNS in AD DS

Active Directory needs DNS. It has to have it available because that's how clients discover their domain controllers in order to logon and search through the Active Directory database. They have to find the Active Directory database; they do so with DNS. Plus DNS has the ability to embed its resource records into Active Directory, and use the Active Directory database as the secure repository to store and replicate the DNS data because it's so vital to a Microsoft network. Installing Active directory will actually automatically install DNS for us on a domain controller, if it's not installed, by default. It enables that functionality whenever you need it. Thus, it is a critical service and it enables, secure dynamic updates, and it enables the ability to use some Microsoft proprietary technologies, it's a good thing to implement. It also is going to still be able to communicate and work with your standard non-Active Directory-integrated DNS whenever you needed to.

9.4: DNS Referrals and Queries

A request of name resolution is sent by a DNS server to another and this process is called referral. It is crucial to complete the DNS process because before reaching to adequate server, DNS has to ask from several servers about the information that is required. It works on sending one query and receiving one reply. There are mainly two types of name resolution requests, as follows:

1. **Recursive query: -** The DNS server is fully responsible to resolve the requested name resolution in a recursive query. DNS Server replies immediately to the requestor and if the server does not have the information about the name then it sends referrals further to different DNS server till does not get the required information. TCP/IP client resolvers generate recursive queries only to their designated DNS servers.

2. **Iterative query: -** DNS server which obtains name resolution request instantaneously responds with the adequate information it holds at that time in iterative query. DNS server exercises iterative queries whiling communicating to each other.

NOTE: - The only time a DNS server sends recursive queries to another server is in the case of a special type of server called a forwarder, which is specifically configured to interact with other servers in this way.

9.5: DNS Components

Let's talk about the moving parts – the DNS components for a moment. You know each DNS server comes with a text file called cache.dns that has the list of root servers on the Internet and those are actually populated in what is known as root hints. We are then going to build our zones, primary zones that are read/write, that have the ability to replicate to secondary zones, that are read-only using a standard zone transfer process or DNS notify, or we can build Active Directory-integrated zones that support Active Directory replication instead of those processes. Normally, our zones are going to be established for the ability to support a specific naming context. But we can also build what are known as global name zones, and these are going to be used for flat lookups and single name lookups without a domain context. The process of lookups again is going to be answered by a recursive query coming from a client to the server. Recursion means use DNS to answer your DNS queries and it's exactly what DNS does.

There are three zone types of DNS server in server 2012. These zones state the location of zone database in the server with kind context it possesses. Zones are briefly mentioned at below.

1. **Primary zone: -** It keeps the master copy of the zone database and allows administrators to make all kind of changes to the records and zone's resources.
2. **Secondary zone: -** it keeps the duplicate copy of the primary zone on either another driver or another server. It is a backup copy of the primary zone database which keeps an identical text file. To make any kind of changes in secondary zone you have to update the resource records in primary zone and can be reflected by a process called zone transfer.
3. **Stub zone: -** It keeps the key resource records of primary zone that recognize the authoritative server for the zone. It forwards or refers the request. The IP address of the host server is associated with stub zone. When the stub zone configured server receives a query for a name in that zone, depending on types of query recursive or iterative, it either forwards the request to the host of the zone or replies with a referral to that host.

But wait, there's more. In addition to what we have been describing, keep in mind that these zones that we build are what we call standard forward lookup zones. That means they turn names into IP addresses. We also have reverse lookup zones that convert IP addresses to names that are used for security and verification processes mainly or for our reporting tools. Each zone is going to have what's called as Start of Authority, or SOA. The Start of Authority record indicates the version number, the primary server, who to e-mail, and how often to refresh your zones. They are used as kinds of rules for a particular zone.

9.6: DNS Records

When you configure your own DNS, you need to create resource record for every host name, so that user can access it over your network. DNS servers utilize different types of resource records and most imperative records are as below.

1. **SOA (Start of Authority): -** Indicates that the server is the best authoritative source for data concerning the zone. Each zone must have an SOA record, and only one SOA record can be in a zone.

2. **NS (Name Server): -** Identifies a DNS server functioning as an authority for the zone. Each DNS server in the zone (whether primary master or secondary) must be represented by an NS record.

3. **A (Address): -** Provides a name-to-address mapping that supplies an IPv4 address for a specific DNS name. This record type performs the primary function of the DNS: converting names to addresses.

4. **AAAA (Address): -** Provides a name-to-address mapping that supplies an IPv6 address for a specific DNS name. This record type performs the primary function of the DNS: converting names to addresses.

5. **PTR (Pointer): -** Provides an address-to-name mapping that supplies a DNS name for a specific address in the in-addr.arpa domain. This is the functional opposite of an A record, used for reverse lookups only.

6. **CNAME (Canonical Name): -** Creates an alias that points to the canonical name (that is, the "real" name) of a host identified by an A record. Administrators use CNAME records to provide alternative names by which systems can be identified.

7. **MX (Mail Exchanger): -**Identifies a system that will direct email traffic sent to an address in the domain to the individual recipient, a mail gateway, or another mail server.

NOTE: - when you install the DNS server, SOA and NS records create by default. Another thing need to notice that PTR record is the part of reverse lookup always.

9.7: Changes to DNS Client in Server 2012

1. Outbound LLMNR (IPv6) queries are not sent to mobile broadband and VPN interfaces.

2. The outbound NETBIOS queries are not sent to mobile broadband interfaces.

3. The LLMNR query timeout has been increased to 410 milliseconds for the first retry and 410 milliseconds for the second retry.

4. The timeout value is now 820 milliseconds.

5. LLMNR and NETBIOS are issued in parallel and optimized for IPv4 and IPv6 queries.

6. Interfaces are divided into network to send parallel DNS queries and prefer binding order responses.

7. A specific interface hijacks DNS names resolution, then for flat names on those networks, LLMNR and NETBIOS queries are sent in parallel with DNS queries and the LLMNR or NetBIOS response is preferred.

8. All the queries in DNS cache service are asynchronous - response timing is therefore optimized.

Summary

- DNS stands for Domain Name System, is a heart of the server to keep it alive over the network. It consists of three elements DNS namespace, name servers and resolvers.

- It follows the hierarchal root architecture in working process. It looks for authoritative DNS server and collects the required information from there and save it to its cache.

- Without DNS an Active Directory cannot be reached by a client as they have to locate domain controllers and they do so with DNS.

- DNS process two types of queries recursive query and iterative query. Client does recursive query to locate information form DNS and DNS servers does iterative query to each other to exchange the required information.

- DNS is a zone oriented service with three types of zones. Primary zone contains master data, secondary zone contains identical copy of primary zone as a backup and stub zone contains key resource record of primary zone which help to locate authoritative server of the zone.

- DNS does forward lookup to locate the IP address from domain name and reverse lookup locates domain name from IP address. Both are the significant for the name conversion and vice versa.

- A DNS server contains mainly seven types of records in its configuration. SOA, NS, A, AAAA, PTR, CN and MX are the records which holds the host information.

- Some new features are also incorporated with the DNS server in server 2012.

Chapter 10

AD DS

Objectives

The following objectives are covered in this chapter:

- Active directory & its multi-master database.
- Active directory components & roles of domain controller.
- Schemas of active directory.
- Roles of DNS in active directory working.
- Supported forest functional level in domain.
- How to install AD DS & upgrade existing DC to server 2012.
- Installation of DC with IFM.
- AD DS on windows Azure.
- Elucidates AD users, computer & OU.
- GUI & command line administrator tools.
- Trust relationship between server & client.
- How to remove installed DC.

Introduction

Active Directory is Microsoft's proprietary implementation of LDAP, the Lightweight Directory Access Protocol. It is Microsoft's central tool for authentication and directory lookup, and the majority of enterprise networks worldwide use some form of directory service in order to allow users to log on to a particular station, and then have centrally defined and controlled access to all those network resources that need to be made available to them. In this day and age, that may then further extend out into the cloud to be able to establish Single Sign-On for remote connections that are available worldwide.

This chapter is about Active Directory Domain Services, setting up the domain controller environment that then will support the centralized authentication, and search capability. And then after installing the service, we will look at the ability to create those core Active Directory objects of users and computers.

10.1: Active Directory Overview

Administrators often choose to build out an Active Directory environment so that they are going to have the opportunity to create a secure boundary - a world in which they know their objects that they maintain, the users that log into the system, the computers from which they log into, or that they access as server systems on this network. The defined levels of access to these resources are going to be guided by this central mechanism of Active Directory, which is a database. It allows you to find what you are looking for and it's a distributed database that allows for authentication, and searches to be made across the globe if that's how far your Active Directory environment stretches, because there will be relative mechanisms used to make sure that process is fast and efficient wherever you have installed the Active Directory for your forest.

10.2: Active Directory: Multi-Master Database

Domain services, Active Directory, when we install this role, we are saying that we want to build this essential database. Ntds.dit is the key file that will be stored, that maintains the collection of users, groups, and computers that we maintain. And as a replicated database, the idea is, you will be able to install the same service within the same security context on other systems, allowing for users whose accounts are stored on any of those domain controllers to be able to authenticate to any of those domain controllers. And then when they need to access a remote resource, that remote resource requires validation. But that validation can be provided across the network based upon the credentials that initially logged on with being revalidated and presented to that remote server.

For the purposes of high-availability, load balancing, and redundancy, it's always best to have at least two domain controllers in your Active Directory design. The initial construction of an Active Directory database of domain services works fine with just one, but having a second one is going to be important both in terms of providing those functionalities, and allowing you the ability to understand what happens in the process of replicating both the elements of the database and physical objects that go along for the ride such as Group Policy files that have to be distributed to each server to enable centralized management of the users throughout the domain.

10.3: Active Directory Components

1. Logical component
2. Physical component

Table 10.1 and 10.2 contain the description of components respectively.

Table 10.1: - Logical components.

Logical Component	Description
Partition	A section of AD DC database. Although the database is one file named NTDS. DIT, it is viewed, managed, and replicated as if it consisted of distinct sections or instances. These are called partitions, which are also referred to as naming contexts.
Schema	Defines the list of object types and attributes that all objects in AD DS can have.
Domain	A logical, administrative boundary for users and computers.
Domain Tree	A collection of domains that share a common root domain and a Domain Name System (DNS) namespace.
Forest	A collection of domain that share a common AD DS.
Site	A collection of users, groups and computers as defined by their physical locations. Sites are useful in planning administrative tasks such as replication of changes to the AD DS database.
OU	OUs are containers in AD DS that provide a framework for delegating.

Table 10.2: - Physical Components.

Physical Component	Description
Domain Controllers	Contain copies of the AD DS database.
Data store	The file on each domain controller that stores the AD DS information.
Global Catalog Servers	Host the global catalog, which is partial, read-only copy of all the objects in the forest. A global catalog speeds up searches for objects that might be stored on domain controllers in a different domain in the forest.
Read-only Domain Controllers (RODC)	A special install of AD DS in a read-only form. These are often used in branch offices where security and IT support are often less advanced than in the main corporate centers.

10.4: Domain Controller Roles

Building up a domain controller, or DC, means that you are providing something that all DCs have in common, which is a place to log on and a place to search Active Directory. But then it turns out that some domain controllers are a little more special. They have extra responsibilities amongst all the domain controllers that might be a part of the domain or of the forest. Some most important roles are as below:

1. Global Catalog
2. Operations master
3. Forest-wide FSMO roles
4. Domain-wide FSMO roles.

For example, we said that domain controllers and users can search for resources across the forest, and that's because there are dedicated domain controllers that not only house all of the accounts of their own domain, but all the accounts of all the domains in the entire forest. Those are called Global Catalog servers providing that universal functionality.

Then we also have certain servers that maintain integrity of the database for certain key operations. We said that in a forest, you can build a domain; you can build another domain that will be pretty important to make sure that you didn't have two separate administrators building the same domain with the same name at the same time on two different servers.

Thus, there is known as a flexible single master operations, or FSMO, role, an operations master that ensures you can't build two domain controllers, or two new domains with the same name twice, or two domain controllers for that matter. So the domain naming master is the name of that. There are five, two that are forest wide, the schema master that ensures that everything in Active Directory has a common blueprint and the domain naming master, and then within each domain, there are three operations masters: a primary domain controller, or PDC Emulator, which ensures integrity of Group Policies, and synchronization of time and passwords, a relative identifier, or RID, master, which ensures that every user gets a unique, unduplicated security ID, and the infrastructure master, which assures that if we have cross domain permissions and group memberships that name to security ID, references are always kept up-to-date. Hence it's important to be aware that these are out there, and it certainly is going to be making a difference in terms of why does it take longer to access one server versus another, what else is going on that server can be related to the extra functionality that it has.

10.5: Active Directory Schema

The active directory schema acts as a blueprint for AD DS by defining the attributes and object classes. There is a single server called the schema master that is the only read/write copy of a portion of the Active Directory database that is distributed to every domain controller in the forest and that is the schema. The schema is the definition of what objects are possible to build. Why is it that we can build a user? Why is it that a user has a first name and a last name, whereas a computer account has an operating system and a location? Because, the classes of objects are defined in the underlying schema and given various different labels, and then the attributes that it's possible to assign two different classes of objects are assigned also in the schema.

This is why users, computers and groups all have a security identifiers, or SIDs, because they have some common classes, whereas a contact, for example, is something different, and although we can have contacts, printers and shared folders in Active Directory, they belong to a different class of object that's going to have different attributes that apply to it.

The schema is not fixed in stone; we mentioned that there is one read/write place where we can manage it the schema master, and we can do so if we are logged on as a member of a specific group called the Schema Admins. Now to change this, though is usually because we are upgrading to a new version of Active Directory with the new operating system, adding something like Exchange or a linked server, and it needs to add attributes to Active Directory to support that Active Directory integrated application. There are mainly three types of schemas in ADDS such as classes, attribute and object, which are mentioned in table 10.3.

Table 10.3: - Schemas of the AD DS.

Classes	Attribute	Object
User	ObjectSID	User
Group	sAMAccount Name	Computer
Computer	Location	
Site	Manager	
	Department	

10.6: Active Directory and Role of DNS

When a user cannot log on to the domain then usually first thing which you should check is "Can user reach your domain name system, or DNS, server?" And if he can, does your DNS server have the information necessary to get the user to Active Directory? DNS is what translates names to IP addresses. But in the case of Active Directory, there is a very specific kind of record called the service locator, or SRV, record that is used to locate the services that Active Directory provides – namely Kerberos for logon, K password for password urgent updates, for the LDAP searches of Active Directory used when we search for computers, search for printers, trying to assign something permissions, and the global catalog used for when we try and search Active Directory rather than just our particular domain.

Thus, whenever we install Active Directory, by default, it attempts to also have that domain controller be a DNS server allowing for that capability of name resolution for the namespace that the Active Directory domain occupies to overlay that DNS space locally. And there are some advantages; Active Directory integrated DNS – when Active Directory stores its service locator records in DNS, DNS can be stored in Active Directory; meaning, it's securely stored, securely replicated, it supports secure updates, and we just get some great performance advantages out of that integration between DNS and Active Directory.

10.7: Domain and Forest Functional Levels

One of the things administrators need to be aware of is that a domain controller running 2012 brought into, for example, an existing environment is able to include itself pretty easily. It does something called Adprep automatically that makes sure that the replication between the down-level domain controllers and this modern one will function well. However, there is a separate option called the functional level.

The functional level describes the oldest domain controller, the most down-level domain controller that domain will support. So if you have got a 2008 domain controller, 2008 R2, and a 2012 domain controller, you are at the 2008 domain functional level. Now you might have a 2003 member server or a Windows 2000 member server, NT4 member server, probably not, but if you did, they would all be compliant as far as the functional level is concerned. Whatever is the lowest functional level of any domain describes the highest functional level of your forest because there is inter forest information, schema values, updates, replication objects, and then there are domain wide replication objects.

Hence, it is important to be aware of your most down-level domain controller at both levels. A great example of this – in Windows 2008 R2 server, there is the introduction of a feature called the Active Directory Recycle Bin and to this day, if you want to use the recycle bin, you need to ensure that your functional level for your particular Active Directory forest is enabled to your 2008 R2 level or you are not going to be able to use that functionality.

10.8: Installing AD DS

1. Use server manager to install.
2. Use powerShell to install.

Now the process of installing Active Directory is relatively straightforward like most roles it begins typically in Server Manager or in the PowerShell environment where we install this role. When we do the installation of the role, typically, it will ask to install the Remote Server Administration, or RSAT, tools that go along with it locally, so we have the administrative tools and the PowerShell cmdlets that are associated with the role post installation. So Install-Windowsfeature, we can reference AD-Domain-Services and put in that we would like to have the tools that go along with it that is one of our switches.

Now a server core localized installation of a domain controller – great example of when to use PowerShell. But in either case, remember that after the installation you are not done because you got the binaries in place, but you still have not, actually, essentially configured that role. Now in our Active Directory environment, we have the ability to do that utilizing the Server Manager and being able to say that we want to configure the role. There will be a nice little Server Manager flag that will prompt us and have us configure the role directly from there or we can utilize the Install-ADDSDomainController or Install-ADDSDomain capability, there are PowerShell installation scripts that go along with that.

NOTE: - Install AD DS databases in different drives for better performance.

10.9: Upgrading DC to Server 2012

Most administrators are bit reticent to trust in that upgrade process because sometimes things go wrong. Thus, it's nice to build out a separate server, and then promote it to being a member server and a domain controller in that domain, allow that Active Directory replication of the entire Active Directory schema and configuration domain and all the information that goes in there, and then decommission the first server. In addition, even single instance roles like Flexible Single Master Operations, or FSMO, roles will automatically migrate over to that second server if it's the only game in town. When you are done, you can end up with something that is all 2012 without having to do an in-place upgrade.

Upgrade Options

1. Introduce new domain controller and promote it alongside existing.
2. Carry out an in-place upgrade.

Considerations

1. In-place upgrade from 32-bit to 64-bit not supported.
2. In-place upgrade to different language not supported.
3. One step, core to GUI and GUI to core not supported (two step required).

Supported Upgrade Paths

Table 10.4: - Upgraded options in server 2012.

Existing DC Operating System	New DC Operating System	Upgrade Type
Server 2008 and 2008 R2 Standard	Server 2012 Standard Server 2012 Enterprise	In-place
Server 2008 and 2008 R2 Enterprise	Server 2012 Enterprise	In-place
Server 2008 and 2008 R2 Datacenter	Server 2012 Datacenter	In-place
Server 2003	Server 2012	Replace

10.10: Install Domain Controllers with IFM

When you are dealing with especially a second domain controller in an existing Active Directory forest, you are going to have to replicate every single user, group, computer, the Active Directory schema, all of your domain information, trust, replication schemes, all the Group Policies, it all has to be replicated. Hence, we have this tool called the **Install from Media**, or IFM. At below, considerations and reasons for using the install from option (IFM) have mentioned.

1. Slow network connections.
2. Reliability of network is a concern.
3. Domain controller is in remote location or branch office.

IFM Process

What you can do is essentially on a functioning domain controller, use the NT Directory Services Utility, or Ntdsutil; it's is a command line utility that you can use to perform an IFM backup. It will create a special snapshot and a backup of your Active Directory database, and if you ask it to the Domain System Volume, or SYSVOL, folder, that holds all of your Group Policies, then you can take that and put it on a network share, pull it down to the other location in an offline way, or you can literally ship it across using a digital video disc, or DVD, or a universal serial bus, or USB drive. Once it has reached the destination, then you can do an installation of Active Directory, put the checkmark into say, **Install from Media** or from the command line, reference the **Install from Media** option, and direct it to the repository of information that has been backed up. And then on boot, it will just synchronize itself with whatever it is out of date with in the current Active Directory environment. It utilizes a backup of AD DS database during installation of DC.

NOTE: - ntdsutil activate ntdsifm create SYSVOL full C:\IFM.

10.11: AD DS on Windows Azure

For fault tolerance and for high-availability, one of the very cool things you can now do in a Windows server 2012 environment is extend your Active Directory domain controller infrastructure into the Windows Azure cloud. To do this, of course, you require an Azure account, and it requires that you build out a virtual machine that will function as the domain controller. You define a gateway to essentially provide a point of entry between your business site and the Windows Azure. And then Active Directory is going to treat Windows Azure as a remote Active Directory site, it has its own site, it has its own subnet, it will have its own rules of replication for how to replicate to Windows Azure. Once you have that networking set of components in place, then you will be able to perform the replication of Active Directory data into that remote environment, elevate that virtual machine to being a domain controller, and perform all the operations that you would normally.

This is why it is Infrastructure as a Service, or IaaS, we are not calling upon Windows Azure to build out a new domain. We are saying, Windows Azure, we want you to host a virtual machine to support my domain. We need your infrastructure, as a service to be provided to me, and that functionality gives us again a higher degree of resiliency, means, you could have your whole site wiped out that is okay, you could rebuild it because that information is up there. You could have cloud components responding to your common Active Directory set of services and elements that are maintained and hosted there in the cloud rather than utilizing the physical resources that are at your site. Thus, extending into the cloud without having to give up the Active Directory that you are already using is a part of what we can do with Windows Azure.

Some significant points have been discussed at below which need to be consider in Windows Azure environment.

1. You need an account on windows azure.
2. It also requires that you build out a virtual machine that will function as the domain controller.
3. AD DS can be deployed into the cloud.
4. Provides method of extending organization reach and boundaries.
5. Can be used to help build more resilient services.
6. May form part of an organization's DR solution.

NOTE: - Active Directory is designed to be able to support intelligent communication by clients and servers in different locales. And that's really what the cloud is; it's a whole different locale.

10.12: AD Users, Computers & OU

When most administrators think about Active Directory, they really think about users and computers nestled in organizational units, or OUs, because that's what our day-to-day administration consists of - managing the account that represent the flesh and blood users, and the nuts and bolts computers, so that they have a stable platform on which to log on, in which they can be controlled by Group Policy, in which they can be administered and passwords are reset, values are defined. Both of these object types have properties that define them.

Users

1. User accounts control user access and privilege in AD.
2. User accounts store defined common and unique attributes for a user.

Computers

1. Share common attributes and relationships as user objects.
2. Computer also authenticate with the domain.
3. Normally grouped and managed using group policy.

OU (Organizational Unit)

Active Directory does not expect us to have just one big flat list of all of our users and groups and computers and printers and shared folders and sites and subnets and servers all just in one place. No, instead there is an expectation that we are going to need to be organized about that, and when it comes to the majority of our day-to-day Active Directory objects - users, groups, and computers, the expectation is that we will be building out organizational units. Now when we look at these logically in Active Directory, they look like a folder and they function like a folder. They create a sub-hierarchy, a path if you will to, where a particular object lives and that's based upon the Lightweight Directory Access Protocol, or LDAP, that the path is specified. Now the advantages of this, why not just have everything at one place? Well makes it easier to find something specific because you look for the OU that has the right location name or maybe the right departmental identifier, maybe it's separating out users and computers, so it's by the function of the resource that's held inside of it, and it just makes it easier to see what is going on.

So also two other extremely important reasons to build organizational units; number one, you can delegate authority. You could take someone who is not a domain admin and is not a standard user and make them an OU admin, full authority if you want over that OU, but not over any other OUs. And that's going to give you the kind of control that you want. The other ability that an organizational unit gives you is the ability to deploy Group Policies to just a set of users, to just the users in the Portland OU because I am pushing to them a proxy server definition that won't make sense for the users in the Denver OU.

1. Containers are used to organize and group objects in a domain
2. Easier to manage than flat container of object
3. OU structure can follow organizational structure

    By function -> Computer, User, Printer

    By Location -> New York, London, Dublin

    By Department -> Sales, Finance, Management

10.13: GUI Based Administration Tools

When we install an Active Directory domain controller, by default, it will add the graphical administrative tools that we often use for our day-to-day work. There are several tools in the server even third party tools to manage services, however, server 2012 contains some tools by default and these are as follows:

1. **Active Directory Users and Computers: -** We'll build out users, and computers, and organizational units, and printers, and shared folders using Active Directory Users and Computers.
2. **Active Directory Sites and Services: -** We have a Microsoft Management Console, or MMC, snap-in also for Active Directory Sites and Services. This is how we control replication and define our boundaries for where a logon should occur.
3. **Active Directory Domains and Trusts: -** We have Active Directory Domains and Trusts, which is where we can see all the domains in the forest and manage the trust

relationships that are used for domains, that are distributed to a great degree within the forest, and need to have a shortcut trust built. But more often when we need to manage external trust, as a business partner or a resource outside of my forest that I need to allow for authentication using the Kerberos protocol.

4. **Active Directory Administrative Center: -** allow me to manage things like Dynamic Access Control, the Active Directory Recycle Bin has some great features for being able to quickly search for accounts and be able to reset their passwords quickly. So it really is designed to be exactly what it says it is, an Administrative Center for the key things that we need to do as admins in our Active Directory environment.

In addition to the graphical tools, of course, we have the ability to manage our Active Directory environment using a set of Active Directory PowerShell cmdlets. Now in addition to the standard graphical tools and the PowerShell tools, Active Directory also comes with a set of what are known as the DS tools, Directory Service command line tools.

10.14: Manage AD DS with Command Line

As administrator lot of times you can get frustrated trying to work with the standard Active Directory Users and Computers when you need to perform a bulk activity. When you have got say 50 users to create a rapid succession, and if you have an awareness of some of the command line tools that can be used to speed this up, you can make your life a lot easier.

CSVDE (Comma-Separated Value Directory Exchange)

You have CSVDE, the Comma-Separated Value Directory Exchange utility, which can be used to import or export a set of accounts in or out of Active Directory. So if you have a file that you could create in Excel, which supports the Comma-Separated Value environment, you can essentially create all the definitions for user accounts that you need first, and then import them in as a single step.

1. Bulk imports and exports of Active Directory objects.
2. Create objects, but does not modify existing ones.
3. Export object and attribute data to CSV file.
4. Use CSVDE to exports to a .csv file.
5. Use CSVDE to create objects from a .csv file.

NOTE: - It will export more attributes then you have the ability to modify. Thus, it will tell you when it was last modified, but you don't get to define last modified as you bring in a new Active Directory object. So watch out for that, you'll get errors otherwise.

LDIFDE (Lightweight Directory Interchange Format Directory Exchange)

The other key command line tool for bulk management of accounts is LDIFDE, the Lightweight Directory Interchange Format Directory Exchange utility. And this command line tool is again used to import, export, and potentially modify on import in a set of Active Directory objects. It uses all the same syntax as csvde to define the file

You also can use LDIFDE, utility, which again allows for import and export, but one of its great tools is it also allows for modification of existing accounts. So you could do an export of say, a set of 17 accounts, and then you could turn around and import those accounts back in modifying their properties to the new values that they need to have. Again because of something like a change in location or a change in other attributes that need to be defined, maybe it's just you all have a new manager, you keep track of that in Active Directory, that's cleanly set that up using this property.

1. Bulk import and export of Active Directory objects.
2. Can create, modify, delete AD objects.
3. Uses LDAP- compliant file format, LDIF.
4. Use ldifde to export objects to a LDIF file.

NOTE: - This tool allows you to not only export and import, but it also allows you to modify existing accounts, which you cannot do with csvde.

DS Commands

So as an Active Directory administrator, we said one of the tools that are available from the command line and have for several generations of the Windows Server operating system are the DS commands. And the most important thing for most administrators to get a handle on is that each of these commands requires the command to be followed by the object type that you are trying to manipulate. For example, dsget user allows to get user properties, dsget computer allows to get computer properties. Also remember that this is a great tool to use with the dsquery tool piping to a dsget or a dsmod command.

10.15: Trust Relationship Between Server and Client

We have discussed about creating computer accounts, but one of the challenges with computer accounts is when we try and log on as a domain user and either Active Directory or the local machine has been reset, maybe by a restore to a checkpoint, a safe state, a backup, any of those situations can cause the system to no longer trust Active Directory, because the machine password has been changed and no longer synchronized with Active Directory. Well that used to require joining a workgroup and then coming back and joining a domain.

But you have a new option available. Now you can essentially log in as either a cached or as a local administrator. You use the local administrator option in this case. And then, there is a PowerShell cmdlet that you can run in a privileged prompt. Thus, you fire your PowerShell here, say; you want to run that as an administrator, absolutely.

And it's a long and complex cmdlet called ***Reset-ComputerMachinePassword***.

When you execute that, need a good name and a password to make that happen in Active Directory. You can use the Get-credential PowerShell cmdlet, which will prompt you then for some Active Directory credentials to send over the network. Finally restart the system and log on. Instead of giving you a problem with the failed password of the machine account connecting that to Active Directory, it lets you log on, because the computer password is correctly synchronized.

10.16: Removing Domain Controller

With Active Directory domain controllers, or DCs, it's easy come and easy go. Being a domain controller is really just a service that's running on a particular system; it's a role that we can install, and then we can uninstall. Now this process, you can drive through either PowerShell cmdlets to remove a system from Active Directory or through the Server Manager. You have essentially the ability to remove the role, which will trigger removing the service of Active Directory first before it removes the role from the system, because it's important that the other domain controllers recognize to stop replicating to this particular domain controller, not allow logons, remove the domain name system, or DNS, record" – all of that needs to be pulled out. And really there is a workflow that you have to be aware of as well because you may simply be removing a duplicate domain controller, because it's no longer needed at a particular location, it's redundant, you want to repurpose the box, and whatever it might be. But then there is also removing an entire domain.

This takes enterprise administrative privileges rather than just domain privileges, and in order to perform that action, you of course need to remove all the domain controllers one by one until you get to the last one. If you are removing multiple domains, keep in mind, you want to work your way from the bottom up or removing child domains before parent domains and removing all domains until you get to the forest root. If you wanted to remove that as well, then of course you remove all the domain controllers and eventually remove the last one, the Active Directory database disappears, never to be seen again, unless you have a very good backup. So this is not something to be taken lightly.

Now you do have the ability to force domain controller removal as well. There is a switch for that, as you use PowerShell cmdlets, and that would be for when you cannot communicate with other domain controller yet you need to repurpose the box to no longer function as a DC. Don't do that except in the most urgent of circumstances because that is going to require some metadata cleanup on the part of the domain controllers still remain because they were never told that DC left the office.

Summary

- LDAP (Lightweight Directory Access Protocol) is the Microsoft proprietary which contains Active Directory services. It provides the central management system to control network and users.

- Active Directory creates a secure boundary and locates a central database in which you can trace the data just like a distributed database.

- When you install the Domain services, a file named Ntds.dit is created which contains the database data. For the redundancy, at least two domain controllers should be in your Active Directory design but having a second one is going to be important both in terms of providing those functionalities, and allowing you the ability to understand what happens in the process of replicating both the elements of the database.

- There are several components in Active Directory which are cartridge on the basis of logical component and physical component.

- Domain Controller perform very crucial role in the network for an administrator such as Domain-wide FSMO role, Global Catalog, Operations Master and Forest-wide FSMO roles.

- The active directory schema acts as a blueprint for AD DS by defining the attributes and object classes. In other word, schema defines the possible objects which can be built.

- Without DNS, you even cannot install the AD DS, thus, it is the mandatory as it contains a very significant record called service locator (SRV). It assists the user or client to locate the domain controller in your forest.

- One day this world might be only with the server 2012 but till that you need to work at least with server 2008 & 2008 R2. Thus, select forest functional level minimum to server 2008. You can ignore server 2003 because Microsoft has stopped support for the same.

- You can install AD DS either by server manager or powerShell. You can also install the AD DS remotely with the help of some tools like RSAT, RDP etc. Up-gradation options are also available but keep in mind that you are selecting the correct path to upgrade.

- There is a tool called IFM (Install From Media) which is used when you decided to install second domain controller in existing Active Directory. It offers the facility to replicate the existing domain controller.

- In contemporary time, all IT infrastructures prefer over cloud network and AD DS is not an exception. For high availability, you can extend your AD DS infrastructure into the windows Azure cloud in server 2012.

- Administrators manage user's accounts and computers in AD DS with the help of OU (organizational Unity). Also, two other extremely important reasons to build organizational units; number one, you can delegate authority. The other ability that an organizational unit gives you is the ability to deploy Group Policies to just a set of users.

- There are numerous other tools (such as Active Directory Users and Computers, Active Directory Sites and Services, Active Directory Domains and Trusts & Active Directory Administrator Center) in GUI which assist an administrator to manage the services in the server 2012.

- You can manage the AD DS with command line as well. Just like GUI tools, CSVDE, LDIFDE and DS commands are some decisive tools in command line environment to manage AD DS.

- There is a new feature in server 2012 which rectify the trust relationship error between server and client. Before that you had to rejoin the domain if the error occurs but now there is a cmdlet command to fix it.

- AD DS is easy to install and easy to go. You can use either server manage or powerShell to remove the AD DS. If you want to remove the Domain Controller completely then you have to remove the services one by one. To perform this operation you need enterprise administrative privileges rather than just domain privileges.

Chapter 11

AD Groups & GPOs

Objectives

The following objectives are covered in this chapter:

- Active Directory groups & its scopes.
- What is group nesting in AD?
- Default groups & enumerating group membership.
- Special identities & permissions.
- What is a group policy?
- GPO links & precedence.
- Role of client group policies.
- How central stores work.
- New feature to update GPOs in server 2012.

Introduction

When you look at Active Directory groups and objects such as Users and Computers, it is important to understand the interdependence that they have with each other and that as an administrator, you need to make sure that you are correctly managing those configurations so that you don't end up with permissions issues, group membership conflicts, things that are going to hamper these user accounts or computer accounts from being able to function in your network environment, and access the resources that they need to access to do their jobs.

Thus, this chapter explains, how to define group nesting, how to convert groups from one scope to another, or one type to another, how to manage and change group memberships, discover what types of groups people belong to and to enumerate groups, and how to delegate group membership management to perhaps managers or other non-IT folk, who need to be able to perform those actions. Then in addition to managing these containers and groups, this chapter also focuses on the ability to work with Group Policy. Now Group Policy is a central tool that you have for being able to control the behavior of how computer accounts and user accounts are able to function in your environment?

11.1: AD Groups

In Active Directory, you have Group Policies which govern the accounts that live in a particular Active Directory path. And an object only lives in one path at a time. Group membership is different though. Group membership is more like membership cards in your wallet. Because every group adds a security unique identifier, or ID, to your user's native ID. Thus, just like you can have a warehouse discount card, a library card and gym membership card, you can have them all simultaneously and kind of whip-out the card that you need at a moment's notice. In the same way, users can belong to multiple groups each one describing what that user should have access to via their group membership.

Now the scope is going to determine membership and visibility and will delve into these, but essentially in Active Directory, you choose from the **Global**, **Domain local**, and **Universal** groups. Then also have the **Security** type. Is it a **Security** group and therefore essentially has the security ID associated with it, and it can be assigned rights and permissions just like a user or computer could? Or is it a **Distribution** group? And its only purpose is to serve as an e-mail distribution group for an Active Directory-integrated e-mail system such as Exchange, where it will appear in the global address list. By the way, a **Security** group does also provide that same distribution list capability for e-mail aware applications where a **Distribution** group only provides that functionality. Next section elucidates in detail about group scopes.

11.2: Active Directory Group Scopes

Default containers simply pass on any Group Policies that are linked to the domain to their members. They do not have the ability to inject any additional policies at that level. The key difference between a container and an OU is the fact that a default container cannot receive separate Group Policies. Below table 11.1, shows the scopes of group.

Table 11.1: Explain scopes of different groups in the forest.

Group Scope	Members from Same domain	Members from Domain in same forest	Members from Trusted external domain	Can be assigned permissions to resources
Local	U, C, GG, DLG, UG and local users	U, C, GG, UG	U, C, GG	On the local computer only
Domain Local	U, C, GG, DLG, UG	U, C, GG, UG	U, C, GG	Anywhere in the domain
Universal	U, C, GG, UG	U, C, GG, UG	N/A	Anywhere in

				the forest
Global	U, C, GG	N/A	N/A	Anywhere in the domain or a trusted domain

U = User

C = Computers

GG = Global Group

DLG = Domain Local Group

UG = Universal Group

11.3: Active Directory Group Nesting

Keep in mind, none of these group scopes are really designed to stand alone. There is a workflow process that really can be used to allow for a consistent level of access which is flexible for new users and new resources to be created overtime and to maintain a level of availability. We call that the Identities, Global groups, Domain local groups, Assigned access to a resource, or IGDLA, acronym.

1. Identities (I): Users or computers are members of.
2. Global groups (G): Which collect members based on members' roles which are members of.
3. Domain local groups (DL): Which provide management, such as resource access.
4. Assigned access to a resource (A): In a multi-domain forest, it is IGUDLA, where U is Universal.

11.4: Default Groups

As administrators, you tend to spend a fair amount of time focused on the needs that you have to build up your own groups. But remember that from the Information Technology, or

IT, side, you need to be carefully monitoring the membership of a couple of the default groups that are built automatically in Active Directory and understand how they function. Details of default groups have been discussed in table 11.2.

Carefully manage the default groups that provide administrative privileges because these groups:

1. Typically have broader privileges that are necessary for most delegated environments.
2. Often apply protection to their members.

Table 11.2: Default groups in AD DS.

Group	Location
Enterprise Admins	Users container of the forest root domain
Schema Admins	Users container of the forest root domain
Administrators	Builtin container of each domain
Domain Admins	Users container of each domain
Server operators	Builtin container of each domain
Account operators	Builtin container of each domain
Backup Operators	Builtin container of each domain
Print Operators	Builtin container of each domain

11.5: Enumerating Group Membership

As an administrator of Active Directory, who is trying to wrestle with why are things working in the way that they are right now? One of the things you may want to do is just quickly be able to spot check group membership. Now locally, if you are logged on as a user and want to check this, often with command line, just use the whoami command with the switch groups, that's find out what groups both directly and indirectly you belong to, directly and through group nesting.

On the other end of the spectrum, you can use the PowerShell cmdlet of get-ADGroupMember and reference an Active Directory group and you will get the membership list. But don't miss out on the recursive switch. If you use the recursive switch, it will dig down, and so what if you check for example, the membership list of an Active Directory Domain local group, it could then show you the membership list including the Universal groups, Global groups, and individual users that are all available through that recursive process of kind of checking and re-checking the list throughout that. Thus, utilize that switch when you really want to drill down and get every possible account that could be referenced as a part of that particular group.

11.6: Special Identities

Sometimes it gets even trickier to try and track down a group that you are looking for, if that group is a special identity. Special identities are different than standard groups, because groups will have a membership list and it is simply very explicit, either you are on the list or you are not, either an administrator put you inside of Domain Admins or they did not, they put you whether you are a member of sales or you are not. But the special identities are reflective of your environment; they say, "Ah, I see that this is true and therefore this group applies to you." It is more like a badge than it is standard group membership, and it is a very dynamically managed system.

Now special identities include anonymous logon which of course would be if you are logging on anonymously, which is very difficult to do actually in a Windows environment, very rarely it is allowed, but there is a special identity to reflect that. Everyone applies essentially the same as authenticated users unless it is weakened to include the anonymous logon service, which again it does not, by default, there is a special property, if that has to be manipulated to allow that to be true.

Interactive refers to a local logon; you are literally sitting at a particular workstation, network says you are not at the local workstation; you are connecting over the network. And Creator owner is a permission that is a group special identity that is used to grant permissions to the particular account that created an object. If you built it, you get special permissions that reflect that. So special identities are circumstance-based, and that is how you want to think about using them. You need to consider below points while providing the special permissions.

1. Are groups for which membership is controlled by the operating system?
2. Can be used by the windows server operating system to provide access to resources.
    I. Based on the type of authentication or connection.
    II. Not based on the user account.
3. Important special identities include:
    1. Anonymous
    2. Authentication logon
    3. Everyone
    4. Interactive
    5. Network
    6. Creator owner

11.7: Permissions

When you work with Active Directory objects, it is important that you recognize that in the same way that we have a hierarchy of objects in a file system and with an NT file system, or NTFS, or Resilient File System, or ReFS, file system that all of those objects have permissions, the same is true in Active Directory.

Active Directory objects, all maintain a discretionary access control list, or DACL, and a system access control list, or SACL, that are used to describe the permissions of those who have access with the discrete list of access control entries, or ACEs, that will say for example, the system has full control, authenticated users have special access. These are individual access control entries. Thus, SACLs and DACLs with ACEs contain security identifiers, or SIDs, of the users and groups that should have access to objects. It is all a part of how Active Directory maintains a secure environment and will allow for the delegation of authority to other administrators. Some significant points have been mentioned at below.

1. Permissions assigned to users and groups accumulate.
2. Best practice is to assign permissions to groups, not to individual users.
3. In the event of conflicts
     I.   Deny permissions override allow permission.
     II. Explicit permissions override inherited permissions
     III. Explicit allow overrides inherited deny.
4. To evaluate effective permissions, you can use
     I.   The effective access tab
     II. Manual analysis

11.8: Group Policies

Active Directory provides you one of the most powerful tools for administration that you could ever hope for, and that is Active Directory Group Policy. Group Policy is a set of files that sit on a domain controller that describe user and computer behavior. And those files are all given identities that are associated with accounts in Active Directory. Those reference accounts are then linked to organizational units, or OUs, and to the domain, and then affect the users that are within those particular containers. Because when a user logs on or a computer boots up, they go to Active Directory and says, "Hey, Active Directory lock me down".

And then when a computer downloads a Group Policy suddenly, it knows how to get its updates, how to setup its firewall, what applications to allow and what user right should be enabled. It can launch scripts, mapped drives, offers network shares and register printers over the network. We can define the way that the user desktop environment should be, mean just all sorts of capabilities - centrally managed and able to be easily manipulated.

Group Policies are divided in their workload into computer settings and user settings. Things that affect a user - that is going to be in the path of this policy and have permissions to receive it, and configuration settings that would apply to a user. The same GPO could have settings for both locations. But some settings apply when the computer boots, if the computer is in the right path. And some apply only when the user logs on, assuming their user is in the correct path. Path is everything.

11.9: GPOs Link

A Group Policy is completely inert and ineffective to do anything to any user or computer until it is linked. Now you can create a Group Policy object, or GPO, linked to a container, that's one way to create them. You can also create them in a Group Policy objects node and then later link them. After that link itself maintains some properties. The link of a Group Policy object enables you to enable or disable a Group Policy just for a particular organizational unit, or OU, which can be great, if it links to other OUs at the same time. A Group Policy object link allows you to also enforce a collection of settings, if necessary, to make it an enforced policy that demands its way be set. In addition, some more significant points which you should remember have been discussed at below.

1. To deliver settings to an object, a GPO must be linked to a container.
2. Disabling a link removes the settings from the container.
3. GPOs can be linked to
     I.   OUs
     II.   Domains
     III. Sites
4. GPOs cannot be linked to
     I.   System containers
     II.   Computers
     III. Users
     IV.   Groups

5. Deleting a link does not delete the GPO.

When GPOs Apply

GPOs come in the process when:

1. Computers settings apply at startup.
2. User settings apply at logon.
3. Polices refers at regular, configurable intervals.
4. Security settings refer at least every 16 hours.
5. Security Settings are so important that they are refreshed every 16 hours with an enforcement, saying that even if nothing is changed, and go lock down the Security Settings just the way they were when we first started up every 16 hours.

Note: By default, every 90 minutes up to two hours, which is actually a Group Policy defined interval that it could be changed, if necessary, the system will double-check.

11.10: GPO Precedence

Site policies get applied first, but then will be overridden by domain policies. Domain policies in your path will be applied next, but they'll be overridden by organizational unit policies. And again, if you take a look at OU and you look at the inheritance, the Active Directory policies go site, then domain, then organizational unit, each one having the chance to override previously applied policies.

Now all the policies work together, they are aggregate. You get the cumulative effect of all their settings. But if for some reason, those settings collide, that's why this Precedence matters. In the case of failure the top precedence will win. However, what if two group policies conflict those are in the same container? That's why we have a Link Order. Whatever you place at the top of the list is going to be the policy with the highest precedence.

11.11: Client Group Policies

Every local machine has the ability to have some Group Policies applied to it before it even joins Active Directory, and that persists even after joined the Active Directory. You can load the Microsoft Management Console, or MMC, console with administrative privileges, and then add your favorite snap-ins here. You have some snap-ins related to Group Policy Object Management, not necessarily one from Active Directory, but a local Group Policy object. You can edit the default local GPO, which has computer settings and user settings in it.

11.12: The Central Store

The vast majority of Active Directory settings are what are known as administrative templates. Administrative Template settings are called out, because literally there is a template of settings stored in Active Directory that an administrator can define, that configure the registry of local machines. The configured registry files actually are a registry.pol file that's downloaded to the client machines. It used to be known as Architecture Description Markup Language, or ADML, or exactly Administrative Template, or ADM, files that were a part of every Group Policy Object, or GPO, which created a lot of redundant administrative tools floating around, bouncing back and forth between clients and service that weren't really necessary. Thus, Microsoft moved to the Administrative Template Xml-Based, or ADMX, and ADML files which are held once on the domain controller and not replicated down to the client. Because they don't need the management, they just need the registry settings.

It is extensible, but every domain controller is holding their own local store of their ADMX and ADML files. You may want there to be a Central Store, so that if you extend the capabilities of Active Directory by adding new ADMX files, then that is consistent. Thus, this is something that you do by just changing or creating a directory inside the SYSVOL folder in the correct location, populating with ADMX files, which then will be automatically detected and replicated to all other domain controllers in that domain, giving you a consistent experience from management. No matter which domain controller you go to edit Group Policy on, these new extensible settings will always be available. Need to consider below points while working with ADMX and ADML files.

1. Is a central repository for ADMX and ADML files?
2. Is stored in SYSVOL?
3. Must be created manually.
4. Is detected automatically by windows operating systems and windows server operating systems.

11.13: New Feature to Update GPOs

Active Directory Group Policy now gives administrators the ability to centrally define that they would like to enforce a **Group Policy Update** on the clients (use gpupdate \force). This is new, and this is essentially the same as the Windows PowerShell cmdlet invoke gpupdate being remotely sent to the clients. Thus, you can call for this option which is **force** Group Policy update on all computers in this. But they will need to support remote management because this is essentially directing a remote PowerShell cmdlet behind the scenes to cause this behavior to work correctly. So, if you have not enabled WinRM and remote management on those desktops, then they will fail.

Summary

- AD groups play very crucial role for an administrator as it provides the different options to control the network and users centrally. It differentiates groups on the basis of global, domain local and universal groups and each users or computer is the part of one of these groups which decides their functionality in the domain.
- Scopes of the Active Directory group varies according to membership types of group for the users and computers, they belong.

- These group scopes do not work independently or stand alone. They work in group nesting manner which is generally called IGDLA (Identities, Global group, Domain Local group, Assigned access to a resource). In addition, in a multi-domain forest it is referred as IGUDLA where U is the Universal.

- You create the different groups and OU but at the same time you have several default groups which need to be managed carefully as these groups contains some especial permissions and membership.

- There is a way to reference your Active Directory group with the help of some tools such as whoami and getADGroupMember commands. Also you can drill down by using recursive process.

- Special identities are different than standard groups in Active Directory as it offers you to provide the exceptional permissions to a particular group in a standard environment.

- Just like NT file system, Active Directory also has hierarchy of objects and permission. DACL (Discretionary Access Control List) and SACL (System Access Control List) are used to describe the permissions of those who have access with the discrete list of access control entries (ACE).

- Group policy is a very powerful tool for administrators to control and describe the behavior of user and computer in the network.

- Without linking a Group Policy is absolutely torpid and unproductive and cannot influence any user and computer. There are several ways to create the GPO and linked to a container.

- GPOs apply when computer settings apply at startup or user settings apply at login. Actually, GPOs get updated at every 90 minutes by default.

- Client systems also have ability to apply GPOs even without joining the domain. It is possible through local group policy which is contains in Microsoft Management Console (MMC).

- Every domain controller holds their own local store for ADMX and ADML file. It is also known as registry.pol file that is downloaded to the client machine. Actually, these files hold the administrative templet setting which is configured by the administrator for central management.

- In server 2012 administrators can use a new feature to update GPOs on the clients. It is like windows PowerShell cmdletgpupdate with a new switch "force" (gpupdate \force).

Chapter 12

Security

Objectives

The following objectives are covered in this chapter:

- Windows security.
- How defense in depth secure network resources.
- Role of security templates & its distribution.
- Types of user rights & security in user add.
- Responsibilities of UAC.
- Auditing polices.
- Function of AppLocker & SRP.
- Windows firewall & GPOs.
- Best security practices in windows environment.

Introduction

When you look at security in a Windows Server 2012 environment, it is important to understand there are a lot of different elements that must be configured correctly to work together in order to make sure that your environment is truly secure. When you configure Security Policies – a core element of Group Policies, you will be able to create some of that secure environment. There are standard Security Policy elements, application restrictions, the Windows Firewall, and if you appropriately set these together to work in unison, you create a correctly locked-down environment.

This chapter examines a variety of different security features offered in Windows Server 2012 Group Policy. These include the User Rights assignment, who can do what, security templates and configuration to be able to roll out settings more quickly, configuring audit policies annotating who did what and when did they do it, defining user account control, the ability to, kind of, change the way the authentication process works. And in order to have that extra click that says, "Yes I did really mean to install this software."

Moreover, this chapter covers at both AppLocker and Software Restriction Policies, which will enforce that software is or is not going to be able to be executed on a particular system. Also focuses on the configuration and deployment of Windows Firewall Settings using Windows Server 2012 Group Policies. Put it all together and these components are going to help you to ensure that your Windows Server 2012 environment is a secure environment, and you will be able to sleep soundly at night.

12.1: Windows Security Overview

As server administrator in a Windows environment, you have a project in front of you which is a never ending project; and that is keeping up with security. Think about the security risks that you face in a Windows-based network? Concentrate on your servers and their physical presence as well. How are they actually defining control to the systems themselves? And you think about how do you access these systems over the network, what protocols? What methods of communication are viable for those and how are you mitigating against unauthorized access using those protocols and a lack of access at all across protocols you don't trust? What type of access control types are you implementing to describe the ability to validate? This is a trusted account access and a trusted resource in a trusted way.

So what are we going to do as administrators? Are we just going to throw up our hands and say it's too hard? Of course not, right? We're going to buck up and do the right thing here, which is to really be cognizant of how we are going to approach protecting a Windows network from the potential risks and vulnerabilities that are out there. It means you really have to figure out, how are you systems vulnerable? What are your assets? How can those assets be attacked? Whether it is network exploits malware, viruses, direct access, and compromising and deleting important files? You need to think about what are your resources, how are they potentially vulnerable, what methods could be used to exploit those vulnerabilities, and who is motivated to perform attacks against the system because threat motives plus exploit methods plus asset vulnerabilities are going to lead to an attack.

Therefore, what do you do to try and limit the damage, create isolation areas, how are you going to quickly inventory, who is in charge of inventorying what, and then going about the process of determining what happened and how to protect it in the future. And of course, in all of this you want to see a blanket of documentation that says, "Here is what we do to protect ourselves, mitigate problems, and to mitigate the scope of problems when they occur, and how are we going to protect ourselves against the next attack." However, we can't protect against everything; there are zero days' exploits that sometimes we are just unable to deal with.

12.2: Defense in Depth

Administrators who are going to protect these golden resources on their network, should implement a defense in depth strategy, which really means you are just going to put so many walls, so many layers which bolsters the protection of whatever resource it is that you are guarding that to try and attack and gain access to that resource. Actually, it is so difficult, it's not worth it. As in the process of trying to do it for someone who is going to make that extra effort and really work through all these different layers, they are going to get caught in this process because we have put up so many boundaries that are going to protect that resource. Thus, to finding the access becomes difficult due to below points. Table 12.1, also elucidate about the different security approaches.

1. Defense in depth uses a layered approach to security.
2. Reduces an attacker's chance of success.
3. Increases an attacker's risk of detection.

Table 12.1: Different security approaches in a network.

Policies, Procedures, and Awareness	Security Documents, User Education
Physical security	Guards, locks, tracking devices
Perimeter	Firewalls, networks access quarantine control
Networks	Network segments, IPsec, Forefront TMG 2010
Host	Hardening, authentication, update management
Application	Application hardening, antivirus
Data	ACLs,EFS, backup/restore procedures

12.3: Security Templates

Within the Active Directory Group Policy environment and within the Local Group Policy environment, we have a node called Security. The computer security settings are actually defined by an information file, or INF, file called the security template. That means you can create a custom Microsoft Management Console, or MMC, to launch the Security Templates snap-in that can actually manage templates separately, and import and export them into various group policies where they are going to have the desired effect.

Thus, security settings that are defined in Security Templates are core settings that for the most part are binding to the machine that they are received by. Some significant templates have been referred below.

1. Account policies
2. Local polices
3. Event log
4. Restricted group
5. System services
6. Registry
7. File system

Distribution of Security Templates

Now, you know that Security Templates are a core part of the component of Group Policy that is going to be used to harden your Server 2012 systems. So how can you manage this little nugget in Group Policy? Actually, you certainly can with the help of below tools.

1. **Group police: -** Simply use the Group Policy Management environment and configure the settings, mean there is nothing wrong with that. In addition, in that environment, you also can, while selecting security, right-click and export our configuration as a security template.

2. **Secedit.exe: -** You also can export and import in local security templates using Secedit.exe, a command line tool.

3. **Security Templates snap-in: -** Also have the ability to load a custom MMC and add the Security Templates snap-in and Security Configuration and Analysis.

4. **Security Configuration and Analysis Wizard: -** The configuration and analysis tool allows taking one or more templates, which again you can browse, review, and build using the templates snap-in as you would like, and compare them with your current settings and possibly apply them as my local settings. So this allows to take one or more templates, build them together into a database which can kind of, aggregate things together and see what the final result might be.

5. **Security Compliance Manager (SCM): -** Now the final tool in this list is the Security Compliance Manager, the SCM. This is a tool that Microsoft has built into the server environment and one that can download the most updated version from the Microsoft website, and I recommend doing this. Now the idea is that SCM, the Security Compliance Manager, is exactly what it sounds like. When in doubt, say, it backwards, it is going to manage compliance with security for your Server 2012 system. It allows you to bring in templates of various security related nature, but it also is going to give you a portfolio, various different baselines for different types of systems; mean, protecting a domain controller is different than protecting a file server or a web server.

12.4: User Rights Types

The user rights are critical. These are the abilities that you have to describe what kinds of actions a particular account can perform on a system. You deploy this with the Group Policy because, again, you have certain types of systems that are going to be similar to one another. You have desktops, laptops, SQL Servers, web servers, file servers, infrastructure servers, and domain controllers. Each of these should be considered separately and you want to look at the capabilities of certain accounts, and what type of account capabilities should be allowed.

The ability of an administrator to manage user rights is important to recognize that these really break down into two types of user rights.

1. **Privileges:** - It refers to a system wide action that you can perform, and usually that is what you think of in terms of user rights, because they are not based upon working in a particular directory, accessing a particular file, instead they are, again, assumed by the system.

NOTE: - If there ever is contention between a privilege and that is granted through a user right and says permission on a particular file, the privilege supersedes that. You could be denied access to a file explicitly but if a user has the right to back it up for example; he will be able to back it up regardless of that permission.

2. **Logon Rights: -** Logon rights refer to the type of access you can have to the system locally or over the network allowed or denied. And so again, those are very explicitly defined and easy to recognize. For instance, login rights cover below points.

Examples:
1. Add workstations to a domain.
2. Allow log on locally.
3. Backup files and directories.
4. Change the system time.
5. Force shutdown from a remote computer.
6. Shutdown the system.

NOTE: - Keep in mind that when it comes to auditing, you have the ability to audit logons and separately from that, you will also have the ability to audit privilege use. And this is exactly what we are talking about, this distinction between the two types of user rights.

12.5: User Add Security

One that is an interesting wrinkle here is the one called Add Workstations to the domain. This one is actually associate with Active Directory, Group Policy, and the default policies that are a part of Active Directory. By default, all authenticated users have this privilege to add workstations to the domain, which then allows them to add up to 10 machines per user account.

12.6: UAC (User Account Control)

User Account Control, UAC, is a tool that we have had since Windows Vista and continues to be available in both, the desktop and server environments, to help protect us from ourselves. Although it is configured as a security option, it is not truly security. It is not going to allow you to do something you normally would not be able to do, it's simply going to make you think about it, that's what UAC is really all about, saying if there is something that takes administrative privilege that would require the membership of your administrative group capability.

It forces you to take the extra step of saying, "Yes I agree, I did want to do that. This was not an application that is running under the hood compromising my environment, I understand I'm installing software, I understand that I'm adding some binaries to the system." Now you have the ability in order to control the degree and the way that UAC functions in your environment. However, it is all really based under the hood, on the fact that when an administrator logs on, there are actually two access tokens that are created. One, that is a standard user access token that doesn't reveal their administrative group membership, and a second access token that includes their administrative group membership. Thus, UAC will say, "Oh, if you need to step up from one to the other, it requires an agreement or perhaps a name and a password in order for that step to actually occur."

UAC allows the following system-level changes to occur without prompting, even when a user is logged on as a local user:

1. Install updates from windows update.
2. Install drivers from windows update or those that are packaged with the operating system.
3. View windows operating system settings.
4. Pair Bluetooth devices with the computer.
5. Reset the network adapter, and perform other network diagnostic and repair task.

12.7: Auditing

Local Policies contain a collection of settings regarding Audit Policy, and administrators are regularly going to come here and enable certain settings to be able to enable content to be written to the Windows security log. You can't over emphasize the importance of enabling auditing correctly. Under auditing means that you don't have the information you need to be able to have any method of recourse in reactive prescriptive actions regarding a vulnerability that has been exposed.

As mentioned this is part of lifecycle, you have to anticipate, be proactive, try and keep things from happening that would go against your security plan and policies. However, weaknesses get discovered as well. You have a chink in your armor. How are you going to bolster your defenses and make sure that you are protected? Well, you need to know what actually happened. And auditing is a huge step in being able to have documentation of what happened, when it happened, where it happened, you may never know why, but you will have the necessary information to start building up a better protection system that militates against that happening again in the future. In some cases, this may also be foundation for litigation against the attacking party. Configure below policy and plan to build up a secure and protected environment.

1. Local polices
2. Audit policy
3. Auditing documentation
4. Better protection system

Auditing implementation

Consider below options while implementing the audit policy in a production environment.

1. Security templates
2. Auditing group policy
3. Documentation

12.8: AppLocker

Beginning with Windows 7 Desktops you have had a utility in Group Policy that enables you to lock down your environment with regard to applications and that is called Application Restriction Policies or AppLocker.

You can control the error messages. You can set this up in an auditing mode if that's what you want. There are a lot of great options to load in bulk configurations through default settings and local detection of applications to speed up the process of enumerating the applications you trust, and get those made available for your users, and blocking out all of the riffraff that you don't want to install on those systems.

However, there is a restriction as to which application environment this works in. Let's say you have Windows 7 Pro and want to configure this kind of lockdown on applications. You can't use AppLocker, you need to use the separate Software Restriction Policies.

Software Restriction Policies (SRP)

1. Apply to everyone on the computer if the policy is computer-based.
2. List out rules based on various parameters, such as the path, the hash, the specific trusted vendor certificate.
3. Possess the ability to apply internet zones from the trusted source.

But you can blend multiple Group Policy Objects, or GPOs, together to have a combination of policies that will have the desired effect. And again, this can be done directly through the graphical environment. There are some PowerShell cmdlets to find out what's going on and validate what you need.

12.9: AppLocker Rule and Precedence

AppLocker is a set of rules that defines which applications are allowed or not allowed, and to whom are they allowed. In the AppLocker environment per type of application, installer, executable, script or packaged app, will have the ability to either enforce or audit the attempt to use a particular application.

The default stands – if we don't bother to configure, audit or enforce, it is going to be essential to enforce the requirement of the policy. But the cool thing is that as you apply your configuration, the rules are cumulative. So if you have a computer in the production department in your domain, the domain has 10 rules and says nothing about enforcing; and then in the production department, you definitely want to, and it says the same thing, "We don't want to enforce it", and it has 35 rules. You have 45 rules and you end up with the default configuration which is lock them down and enforce it.

12.10: Windows Firewall

Remember the day when the Windows XP Service Pack 2 firewall dropped like a bomb onto the networks because applications were breaking, people were getting frustrated. And it had a great little option built into the firewall - turn off if you are able to disable the policy, if you wanted to; or to lock it down so that everything was protected in case you are. In our more recent environments, the Windows Advanced Firewall and the firewall that you have in your current desktop and server environments, is a little smarter. It allows categorizing the networks into public, private, and domain-based networks as well as exposing applications and ports in recognized networks.

You can control the rules according to different standards and have the ability to configure Internet Protocol Security, or IPSec, based rules also. Don't punch a hole through your firewall, put a locked door in your firewall that only those with the correct key can use to get through as a firewall exception. This is a much more secure way to define your standard for your internal networks to be truly protected because there is always that concern about an insider threat that this can help to mitigate.

12.11: Firewall and GPOs

One of the challenges when it comes to managing the firewall is managing it in the right way or not. You do have, at a local level, the ability to configure the Windows Firewall through a Control Panel. This will give you the ability to define basic port exceptions for inbound access to enable or disable the firewall at private, public, and domain levels. Your more advanced options, to be able to control the firewall and to control behavior such as IPsec rules and configuration, inbound and outbound configurations, to configure security connection rules, to create zones of isolation, all of that is going to be done through the Advanced Windows Firewall Configuration, which is a Microsoft Management Console, or MMC, and a separate tool.

You could drive that locally but, the exact same settings are available to drive centrally through Group Policy. Here is an organizational unit, or OU, it contains a set of servers. Set their firewalls to make exceptions for the ports that those types of servers would need, lock down everything; no one should be accessing. Same thing for desktop, Laptops, maybe it is a little bit different but you configure the firewalls appropriately for those environments.

Do we merge rules? Now this is extremely important and notice the default behavior is **Yes**, you can merge the firewall rules and connection security rules that are used for isolation with the domain rules. Now if you say **No**, that means it is going to be Group Policy standard you can't configure and you won't be able to configure anything locally, so that is an important definition you need to choose. Is it 100% Group Policy managed or is there an option for local merging? The default is a merged setting where the Group Policy standard will override if there are any conflicting settings, but in general, all the rules will merge together.

12.12: Security Practice

Some best practices for increasing security are:
1. Apply all available security updates quickly.
2. Follow the principle of least privilege.
3. Restrict console login.
4. Restrict physical access.

Summary

- In windows environment, security is a very crucial part for an administrator as there are numerous vulnerabilities which can cause potential risk. Server 2012 is not an exception, it is also a part of it and to protect it you have to build a very strong security policy for your network.

- Defense in depth is a strategy which suggests building so many layers to protect your resources over the network.

- Security templates snap-in offers flexible and quickest environment for the administrators to create different policies as they can import and export them wherever they need it. They do not have to create same policies again and again in a domain.

- User rights are very vital aspect in the production environment. Privilege and logon rights are the two types of user rights which can be deployed with the help of GPOs.

- Once a user is Active Directory user then he gets the privilege to add up to 10 machines in the directory. By default, all authenticated users have this privilege.

- UAC (User Account Control) is nothing just a way to provide the administrator rights to legitimate user when he requires. Even a user who belongs to administrator group needs to ask for a token from UAC before performing an administrator activity.

- Auditing settings are necessary to keep monitoring the activities which take place on the server or system. You can set various types of auditing policies in server 2012 to know adequate information in case of any failure and attack.

- You can control the applications through AppLocker. It stands for Application Restriction Policies which can lock the application for a particular user. Administrators can control the user profile with AppLocker. However, it has environment restriction as it can function merely in win 7 and 8 environment for other OS use SRP (Software Restriction Policies).

- Windows firewall is not new as it has been protecting the networks since windows XP SP 2. In the beginning it was quite frustrating but recent environments offer windows advance firewall which divide entire network into public, private and domain-based networks.

- Through the control panel, you can control the firewall which is the easiest way. However, GPOs also offer the firewall setting and it is the preferable method. Moreover, you can merge the both local and GPOs firewall settings and also GPOs firewall settings get preference over local settings.

New Features of Server 2012

1. Multiserver support in Server Manager: - Windows Server 2012 features a completely redesigned Server Manager. It's no longer oriented toward single-server management as it is in Windows Server 2008 R2. Because it embraces the cloud concept, the new Server Manager can manage multiple servers, and it provides an all-new dashboard that lets you drill down into local and remote servers.

2. Server Core is the default: - Windows Server 2012 uses the minimalist Server Core as the default server environment, marking a huge change away from dependence on the GUI for management. One super feature of this change is that the GUI is now considered a feature. Therefore, you can perform your initial server configuration through the GUI, and then remove it when you're ready to move into production. Unlike Server 2008 R2, there's no need to reinstall the OS to get rid of the GUI.

3. Ubiquitous PowerShell management: - Going hand-in-hand with the move away from the GUI is the move to PowerShell as the primary management tool. Server 2008 R2 started this trend and provided more than 200 cmdlets for server management. Windows Server 2012 expands the available cmdlets to more than 2,300, providing cmdlets for managing all Windows Server applications. For instance, Server 2008 R2 doesn't have built-in cmdlets for Hyper-V, but Windows Server 2012 provides a full set of PowerShell cmdlets for managing Hyper-V 3.0.

4. Built-in NIC teaming: - Another overdue feature is the capability to provide NIC teaming natively in the OS. VMware's ESX Server has provided NIC teaming for some time. Prior to Windows Server 2012, you could get NIC teaming for Windows only via specialized NICs from Broadcom and Intel. The new built-in Windows Server 2012 NIC teaming works across heterogeneous vendor NICs and can provide support for load balancing as well as failover over NICs from different vendors.

5. Data deduplication: - Windows Server 2012 provides built-in data deduplication, a feature typically found in high-end SANs. Windows Server 2012's data deduplication runs in the background, and it can automatically detect duplicate data, save the duplicated data in a separate system store, and replace the data in the original files with pointers to the system store.

6. Expanded cluster scalability: - Windows Failover Clustering has also taken a big jump in scalability. VMware's vSphere supported clusters consisting of up to 32 hosts. Previous versions of Windows Server were limited to 16 nodes. Windows Server 2012 clusters can support up to 63 nodes and up to 4,000 virtual machines (VMs) per cluster, effectively leap-frogging VMware's VM cluster support.

7. Multiple concurrent Live Migrations: - Live Migration was introduced with Hyper-V 2.0, which was part of the Server 2008 R2 release. Although it filled an important gap, it lagged behind VMware's VMotion because Hyper-V 2.0 could perform only one Live Migration at a time; VMware's ESX Server could perform multiple concurrent VMotions. Hyper-V 3.0 brings that same ability to Windows Server 2012 and the next release of Hyper-V Server as well.

8. Storage Live Migration: - The addition of Storage Live Migration to Hyper-V 3.0 really closes the feature gap with VMware. Like VMware's Storage VMotion, Hyper-V 3.0's Storage Live Migration lets you move a VM's virtual disk, configuration, and snapshot files to a new storage location with no interruption of end-user connectivity to the VM.

9. Live Migration without shared storage: - Unexpectedly, Microsoft really carved out a clear advantage in the small-to-midsized business virtualization market by introducing the ability to perform Live Migration and Storage Live Migration without requiring shared storage on the back end. The ability to perform Live Migration without a SAN back end helps bring the advantages of virtualization and high availability to smaller businesses that can't afford the cost or complexities of a SAN.

10. Better Edition, SKU Selection: - Kudos to Microsoft for cleaning up what was a muddy value proposition. The core OS is now the same, and the edition you buy—Standard or Datacenter—depends on whether you want to run up to two virtual machines as guests or if you'd like unlimited guest virtualization. There's no Enterprise edition gumming up the works. This is a big win for everyone.

11. Storage Spaces & Flipping Complexity on Its Head: - Storage Spaces is an innovative feature that basically takes commodity storage hardware—inexpensive drives and their controllers, like a JBOD (informal parlance for Just a Bunch of Disks—and turns it into a pool of storage that is divided into spaces that are in turn used just like regular disks.

Each of these pools can contain hot standby disks, and each of the Spaces in the pool can have availability policies such as mirroring and RAID-style redundancy. You can even perform thin provisioning, which is specifying a volume that's bigger than you actually have space for. That way, when you do need the additional room, just pop in a few more drives; no reconfiguration is required. It takes the complexity and expense of network-attached storage and SANs and basically flips it on its head. You can just get a bunch of disks together and get really flexible in carving them up where you need additional space.

12. DirectAccess (A VPN without the Pain of a VPN): - DirectAccess allows VPN-like secure tunneling from any endpoint back to the corporate network without the overhead and performance hit of a true VPN. There is also no management agent on the client. When the technology is configured correctly, it just works—users have seamless connectivity to file shares, on-premises equipment and other resources just as if they were on the corporate campus. In addition, group policy objects get applied and administrators can manage machines wherever they are, not just when they come to headquarters or when they connect up to the VPN. This technology had previously been difficult to set up, but in Windows Server 2012, it very much just works.

13. Dynamic Access Control (New Way of Thinking): - Dynamic Access Control (DAC) is a suite of facilities that really enhances the way you can control access to information. It's no longer about taking files or folders and making decisions about "Yes, these people can" and "No, these people can't."

Instead, it's about abstracting away the individual data and making larger assignments about the types of data that live on your system, as well as the types of users that should and should not have access to it. It's a new way of thinking that very much complements the strong abilities of the file system to secure data. There are minimal schema additions to make to Active Directory, and you can begin using the lion's share of the feature set of DAC with just a Windows Server 2012 file server and a domain controller.

14. Resilient File System (An Evolution of NTFS): - The Resilient File System (ReFS) was designed as an evolution of the New Technology File System (NTFS) with a focus on availability and integrity. ReFS writes to different locations on disk in an atomic fashion, which improves data resiliency in the event of a power failure during a write, and includes the new "integrity streams" feature that uses checksums and real-time allocations to protect the sequencing and access of both system and user data.

Problems identified by Windows Server 2012 on volumes protected with these features can be automatically repaired without bringing the disk or volume offline in most cases—and in many cases without any administrative intervention either. ReFS is also built to scale further than NTFS as well, which is an important point in the age of big data and private cloud operations.

15. Out-of-the-Box IP Address Management: - In the box with Windows Server 2012, you will find a complete IPAM suite. This is something many medium-sized businesses simply don't have access to. With the IPAM suite, you can allocate, group, issue, lease and renew IP addresses in an organized fashion, as well as integrate with the in-box DHCP and DNS servers to discover and manage devices already on your network. If you have not played with IPAM services from

Nortel and others, this is a very interesting and worthwhile inclusion to the product—and, as it's free with the OS license, it's well worth the price.

16. Diskless boot: - Everything that can be moved out of a server, reduces the power and cooling costs. In large complex environments, removing the hard disk out of the server and booting across the network has not only saved money but made the data centre more flexible. Now Windows Server 2012 supports diskless boot as an OS feature. The savings are not just about removing unwanted hard disks from servers, there are also advantages from a management perspective.

For example, an administrator who wants to create a master image for his web servers can just download that image whenever he needs an additional web server. The management saving is that you only patch and maintain the master image, not each installation.

17. NFS 4.1: - Microsoft's **NFS 4.1** server is good code. Designed from the ground up it is fast, stable and reliable. It makes a great storage system for heterogeneous environments and a wonderful network storage point for VMware servers.

18. SMB 3.0: - SMB 3.0 is the crown jewel of Server 2012. It is far removed from its laughingstock predecessor CIFS. It supports multiple simultaneous network interfaces – including the ability to hot-plug new interfaces on the fly to increase bandwidth for large or complex transfers – and supports MPIO, thin provisioning of volumes and deduplication (assuming the underlying storage is NTFS).

SMB 3.0 also supports SMB Direct and remote direct memory access, the ability for appropriately kitted systems to move SMB data directly from one system's memory to the other, bypassing the SMB stack. This has enabled Microsoft to hit 16GBPS transfer rates for SMB 3.0, a weighty gauntlet for any potential challenger to raise.

19. iSCSI: - With Windows Storage Server 2008, Microsoft first made an iSCSI target available. It eventually became an optional download from Microsoft's website for Server 2008 R2 and is now finally integrated into Server 2012 as a core component.

Interview Aid

AD DS & GPOs

Questions & Answers

Questions:

1. What is the release date of server 2012?

2. What is domain?

3. What do you mean by domain controller?

4. What do you mean by Active Directory?

5. Explain three main features of Active Directory?

6. What do you mean by Active Directory functional levels? How does it help an organization's network functionality?

7. What are the Domain and Forest functional levels of Windows Server 2003 AD?

8. What are the Domain and Forest functional levels of Windows Server 2008 AD?

9. How to add additional Domain Controller in a remote site with slower WAN link?

10. How do we install Active Directory in Windows 7 Computer?

11. What are the prerequisites to install Active Directory in a Server?

12. What is FSMO role? (Or what are Single Master Operations / Flexible Single Master Operations / Operations Master Role / SMO / OMR?)

13. Explain Infrastructure Master Role. What will be the impact if DC with Infrastructure Master Role goes down?

14. What are the two forest specific FSMO roles?

15. Which FSMO role directly impacting the consistency of Group Policy?

16. To promote a new additional Domain Controller in an existing domain. Which are the groups a user should be a member of?

17. Tell one easiest way to check all the 5 FSMO roles.

18. Can we configure two RID masters in a domain?

19. Can we configure two Infrastructure Master Role in a forest? If yes, please explain.

20. What will be the impact on the network if Domain Controller with PDC Emulator crashes?

21. What are the physical components of Active Directory?

22. What are the logical components of Active Directory?

23. What are the Active Directory Partitions? (Or what are Active Directory Naming Contexts? Or what is AD NC?)

24. What is group nesting?

25. Explain Group Types and Group Scopes?

26. What is the feature of Domain Local Group?

27. How will you take Active Directory backup?

28. What are the Active Directory Restore types?

29. How is Authoritative Restore different from non-Authoritative Restore?

30. Explain, how to restore Active Directory using command line?

31. Tell few switches of NTDSUTIL command.

32. What is a tombstone? What is the tombstone lifetime period?

33. What do you understand by Garbage Collection? Explain.

34. What is Lost and Found Container?

35. Where can we locate Lost and Found Container?

36. Is Lost and Found Container included in Windows Server 2008 AD?

37. Have you ever installed Active Directory in a production environment?

38. Do we use clustering in Active Directory? Why?

39. What is Active Directory Recycle Bin?

40. What is RODC? Why do we configure RODC?

41. How do you check currently forest and domain functional levels? Say both GUI and Command line.

42. Explain Knowledge Consistency Checker (KCC)

43. What are the tools used to check and troubleshoot replication of Active Directory?

44. What is SYSVOL folder used for?

45. What is the use of Kerberos in Active Directory? Which port is used for Kerberos communication?

46. Which version of Kerberos is used for Windows 2000/2003 and 2008 Active Directory?

47. Please name few port numbers related to Active Directory.

48. What is an FQDN?

49. Tell few DS commands and its usage.

50. Explain Active Directory tree and forest.

51. What are Intersite and Intrasite replication?

52. What is shortcut trust?

53. What is selective Authentication?

54. Give brief explanation of different types of Active Directory trusts.

55. Have you heard of ADAC?

56. What is the use of ADSIEDIT? How do we install it in Windows Server 2003 AD?

57. User is unable to create a Universal Security group in his Active Directory? What will be the possible reason?

58. What is ADMT? What is it used for?

59. What do you mean by Lingering Objects in AD? How to remove Lingering Objects?

60. Explain Global Catalog. What kind of AD infrastructure makes most use of Global Catalog?

61. Global Catalog and Infrastructure master roles cannot be configure in same Domain Controller. Why?

62. How do you check all the GCs in the forest?

63. How many objects can be created in Active Directory? (both 2003 and 2008)

64. Can you explain the process between a user providing his Domain credential to his workstation and the desktop being loaded? Or how the AD authentication works?

65. What is LDAP?

66. Which is default location of Active Directory? What are the main files related to AD?

67. In a large forest environment, why we don't configure all Domain Controllers as GCs?

68. What is NETDOM command line tool used for?

69. What is role seizure? Who do we perform role seizure?

70. What is ISTG? What is role of ISTG in Active Directory?

71. Is it possible to find idle users who did not log in for last few months?

72. What is GPO?

73. What are GPOs (Group Policy Objects)?

74. Tell the order of GPO as it applied.

75. What are the uses of CSVDE and LDIFDE?

76. What are the differences between a user object and contact object?

77. What do you mean by Bridge Head server?

78. What is urgent replication?

79. Please explain Realm trust.

80. Explain object class and object attribute.

81. My organization wants to add new object attribute to the user object. How do you achieve it?

82. What do you understand about GUID?

83. What is the command used for Domain Controller decommissioning?

84. Have you ever planned and implemented Active Directory infrastructure anywhere? Tell few considerations we have to take during the AD planning.

85. Name few differences from Windows Server 2003 AD and Windows Server 2008 AD.

86. Which domain and forest functional level you will select if you are installing Windows Server 2008 AD in an Existing environment where you have Windows Server 2003 Domain Controllers?

87. What are the replication intervals for Intersite and intrasite replication? Is there any change in 2003 and 2008?

88. To transfer RID master role to a new Domain Controller. What are the steps you need to follow?

89. Tell few uses of NTDSUTIL commands?

90. Name few services that directly impact the functionality of Domain Controller.

91. You said there are 5 FSMO roles. Please explain what will be the impact on the AD infra if each FSMO roles fails?

92. What is Active Directory defragmentation? How do you do AD defragmentation? And why do we do it?

93. Tell Different between online and offline defragmentation.

94. How do you uninstall active directory? What are the precautions we have to take before removing active directory?

95. A user is unable to log into his desktop which is connected to a domain. What are the troubleshooting steps you will consider?

96. A Domain Controller called ABC is failing replication with XYZ. How do you troubleshoot the issue?

97. A user account is frequently being locked out. How do you investigate this issue? What will be the possible solution suggest the user?

98. Imagine you are trying to add a Windows 7 computer to Active Directory domain. But it's showing an error 'Unable to find Domain Controller'. How will you handle this issue?

99. What are the services required for Active Directory replication?

100. What is Active Directory application partition? What are the uses of it?

101. Many users of a network are facing latency while trying to log into their workstations. How do you investigate this problem?

102. What do you mean by IDA? What are the new components of Windows 2K8 Active Directory?

103. To edit the Active Directory Schema. How can we bring Schema editor into my MMC?

104. Name few Active Directory Built in groups.

105. What are the differences between Enterprise Administrators and Domain Administrators groups?

106. You have to create 1000 user objects in Active Directory domain. How can you achieve that with least administrative effort? Tell few tools that you can use.

Answers:

1. The RTM version was released in August 2012 and this version is fully supported.

2. A domain is defined as a logical group of network objects (computers, users, devices) that share the same Active Directory database. A tree can have multiple domains. A domain controller allows system administrators to grant or deny users access to system resources, such as printers, documents, folders, network locations, etc., via a single username and password.

3. A domain controller (DC) or network domain controller is a Windows-based computer system that is used for storing user account data in a central database. It is the centre piece of the Windows Active Directory service that authenticates users, stores user account information and enforces security policy for a Windows domain.

4. Active Directory provides a centralized control for network administration and security. Server computers configured with Active Directory are known as domain controllers. Active Directory stores all information and settings for a deployment in a central database, and allows administrators to assign policies and deploy and update software.

5. Active Directory enables single sign on to access resources on the network such as desktops, shared files, printers etc. Active Directory provides advanced security for the entire network and network resources. Active Directory is more scalable and flexible for administration.

6. Functional levels help the coexistence of Active Directory versions such as, Windows NT, Windows 2000 Server, Windows Server 2003 and Windows Server 2008. The functional level of a domain or forest controls which advanced features are available in the domain or forest. Although lowest functional levels help to coexist with legacy Active Directory, it will disable some of the new features of Active Directory. But if you are setting up a new Active Directory environment with latest version of Windows Server and AD, you can set to the highest functional level, thus all the new AD functionality will be enabled.

7. Windows Server 2003 Domain Functional Levels: Windows 2000 mixed (Default), Windows 2000 native, Windows Server 2003 interim, and Windows Server 2003. Forest Functional Levels: Windows 2000 (default), Windows Server 2003 interim, Windows Server.

8. Windows Server 2008 Domain Functional Levels: Windows 2000 Native, Windows Server 2003, Windows Server 2008, Windows Server 2008 R2.Forest Functional Levels: Windows 2000, Windows Server 2008, Windows Server 2008 R2.

9. It is possible to take a backup copy of existing Domain Controller, and restore it in Windows Server machine in the remote locations with slower WAN link.

10. Active Directory is designed for Server Operating System, and it cannot be installed on Windows 7.

11. Windows Server Operating System. Free hard disk space with NTFS partition. Administrator's privilege on the computer. Network connection with IP address, Subnet Mask, Gateway and DNS address. A DNS server that can be installed along with first Domain Controller. Windows Server installation CD or i386 folder.

12. Flexible Single-Master Operation (FSMO) roles, manage an aspect of the domain or forest, to prevent conflicts, which are handled by Single domain controllers in domain or forest. The tasks which are not suited to multi-master replication, There are 5 FSMO roles, and Schema Master and Domain naming master roles are handled by a single domain controller in a forest, and PDC, RID master and Infrastructure master roles are handled by a single domain controller in each domain.

13. Infrastructure master role is a domain-specific role and its purpose is to ensure that cross-domain object references are correctly handled. For example, if you add a user from one domain to a security group from a different domain, the Infrastructure Master makes sure this is done properly. Infrastructure master does not have any functions to do in a single domain environment. If the Domain controller with Infrastructure master role goes down in a single domain environment, there will be no impact at all. Whereas, in a complex environment with multiple domains, it may impact creation and modification of groups and group authentication.

14. Schema Master Role and Domain Naming Master role.

15. PDC Emulator

16. You should be a member of Enterprise Admins group or the Domain Admins group. Also you should be member of local Administrators group of the member server which you are going to promote as additional Domain Controller.

17. Use netdom query /domain:YourDomain FSMO command. It will list the entire FSMO role handling domain controllers.

18. No, there should be only one Domain Controller handling RID master role in a Domain.

19. There should be only one Domain Controller handling Infrastructure master role in a domain. Hence if you have two domains in a forest, you can configure two Infrastructure masters, one in each domain.

20. If PDC emulator crashes, there will be immediate impact on the environment. User authentication will fail as password changes won't get effected, and there will be frequent account lock out issues. Network time synchronization will be impacted. It will also impact DFS consistency and Group policy replication as well.

21. Domain controllers and Sites. Domain controllers are physical computers which are running Windows Server operating system and Active Directory data base. Sites are a network segment based on geographical location and which contains multiple domain controllers in each site.

22. Domains, Organizational Units, trees and forests are logical components of Active Directory.

23. Active Directory database is divided into different partitions such as Schema partition, Domain partition, and Configuration partition. Apart from these partitions, we can create Application partition based on the requirement.

24. Adding one group as a member of another group is called 'group nesting'. This will help for easy administration and reduced replication traffic.

25. Group types are categorized based on its nature. There are two group types: Security Groups and Distribution Groups. Security groups are used to apply permissions to resources where as distribution groups are used to create Exchange server email

communication groups. Group scopes are categorized based on the usage. There are three group types: Domain Local Group, Global Group and Universal Group.

26. Domain local groups are mainly used for granting access to network resources. A Domain local group can contain accounts from any domain, global groups from any domain and universal groups from any domain. For example, if you want to grant permission to a printer located at Domain A, to 10 users from Domain B, then create a Global group in Domain B and add all 10 users into that Global group. Then, create a Domain local group at Domain A, and add Global group of Domain B to Domain local group of Domain A, then, add Domain local group of Domain A to the printer(of Domain A) security ACL.

27. Active Directory is backed up along with System State data. System state data includes Local registry, COM+, Boot files, NTDS.DIT and SYSVOL folder. System state can be backed up either using Microsoft's default NTBACKUP tool or third party tools such as Symantech NetBackup, IBM Tivoli Storage Manager etc.

28. There are two types of Active Directory restores, Authoritative restore and Non-Authoritative restore.

29. Non-Authoritative means, a normal restore of a single Domain controller in case that particular domain controller OS or hardware crashed. After non-authoritative restoration completed, compares its data base with peer domain controllers in the network and accepts all the directory changes that have been made since the backup. This is done through multi master replication. Whereas, in Authoritative restore, a restored data base of a Domain controller forcefully replicated to all the other domain controllers. Authoritative restore is performed to recover an active directory resource or object (eg. an Organizational Unit) which accidentally deleted and it needs to be restored.

30. We can use NTDSUTIL command line to perform Authoritative restore of Active Directory. First, start a domain controller in 'Directory Service Restore Mode'. Then, restore the System State data of Domain controller using NTBACKUP tool. This is non-authoritative restore. Once non-authoritative restore is completed, we have to perform

authoritative restore immediately before restarting the Domain Controller. Open command prompt and type NTDSUTIL and enter, then type authoritative restore and press enter, then type restore database and press enter, click OK and then click Yes. This will restore all the data in authoritative restore mode. If you want to restore only a specific object or sub-tree, you can type below command instead of 'restore database'. restore subtree ou=OU_Name,dc=Domain_Name,dc=xxx

31. Authoritative restore, Configurable settings, Partition management, Set DSRM Password etc.

32. A tombstone is a container objects for deleted items from Active Directory database, even if objects are deleted, it will be kept hidden in the active directory data base for a specific period. This period is known as tombstone lifetime. Tombstone lifetime is 180 days on Windows Server 2003 SP1 and later versions of Windows Server.

33. Garbage collection is a process of Active Directory. This process starts by removing the remains of previously deleted objects from the database. These objects are known as tombstones. Then, the garbage collection process deletes unnecessary log files. And the process starts a defragmentation thread to claim additional free space. The garbage collection process is running on all the domain controllers in an interval of 12 hours.

34. In multi-master replication method, replication conflicts can happen. Objects with replication conflicts will be stored in a container called 'Lost and Found' container. This container also used to store orphaned user accounts and other objects.

35. Lost and Found container can be viewed by enabling advanced features from View menu of Active Directory User and Computers MMC.

36. Yes, it is included.

37. [Never say no] We had set up an additional domain for a new subsidiary of the firm, and I was a member of the team who handled installation and configuration of domain controllers for the sub domain. [or] I was supporting an existing Active Directory network environment of the company, but I have installed and configured Active Directory in test environment several occasions.

38. No one installs Active Directory in a cluster. There is no need of clustering a domain controller. Because Active Directory provides total redundancy with two or more servers.

39. Active Directory Recycle bin is a feature of Windows Server 2008 AD. It helps to restore accidentally deleted Active Directory objects without using a backed up AD database, rebooting domain controller or restarting any services.

40. Read only domain controller (RODC) is a feature of Windows Server 2008 Operating System. RODC is a read only copy of Active Directory database and it can be deployed in a remote branch office where physical security cannot be guaranteed. RODC provides more improved security and faster log on time for the branch office.

41. To find out forest and domain functional levels in GUI mode, open ADUC, right click on the domain name and take properties. Both domain and forest functional levels will be listed there. TO find out forest and domain functional levels, you can use DSQUERY command.

42. KCC can be expanded as Knowledge Consistency Checker. It is a protocol process running on all domain controllers, and it generates and maintains the replication topology for replication within sites and between sites.

43. We can use command line tools such as repadmin and dcdiag. GUI tool REPLMON can also be used for replication monitoring and troubleshooting.

44. SYSVOL is a folder exits on each domain controller, which contains Active Directory related files and folders. SYSVOL mainly stores important elements of Group Policy Objects and scripts, and it is being replicated among domain controllers using File Replication Service (FRS).

45. Kerberos is a network authentication protocol. Active Directory uses Kerberos for user and resource authentication and trust relationship functionality. Kerberos uses port number 88.

46. All versions of Windows Server Active Directory use Kerberos 5.

47. Kerberos 88, LDAP 389, DNS 53, SMB 445.

48. FQDN can be expanded as Fully Qualified Domain Name. It is a hierarchy of a domain name system which points to a device in the domain at its left most end. For example in system.

49. Dsadd - to add an object to the directory, Dsget - displays requested properties of an object in AD, Dsmove - Used to move one object from one location to another in the directory, DSquery - To query specific objects.

50. A tree in Active Directory is a collection of one or more domains which are interconnected and sharing global resources each other. If a tree has more than one domain, it will have contiguous namespace. When we add a new domain in an existing tree, it will be called a child domain.

   A forest is a collection of one or more trees which trust each other and sharing a common schema. It also shares common configuration and global catalog. When a forest contains more than one tree, the trees will not form a contiguous namespace.

51. Replication between domain controllers inside a single site is called Intrasite replication, where as replication between domain controllers located in different sites is called Intersite replication. Intrasite replication will be very frequent, where as Intersite replication will be with specific interval and in a controlled fashion just to preserve network bandwidth.

52. Shortcut trust is a manually created transitive trust which is configured to enable fast and optimized authentication process. For example, If we create short cut trust between two domains of different trees, they can quickly authenticate each other without traveling through the entire parent domains. Short cut trust can be either one-way or two-way.

53. Selective authentication is generally used in forest trust and external trusts. Selective authentication is a security setting which allows administrators to grant access to shared resources in their organization's forest to a limited set of users in another organization's forest. Selective authentication method can decide which groups of users in a trusted forest can access shared resources in the trusting forest.

54. Trusts can be categorized by its nature. There can be two-way trust or one-way trust, implicit or explicit trust, transitive or non transitive trust. Trust can be categorized by types, such as parent and child, tree root trust, external trust, realm trust forest trust and shortcut trust.

55. ADAC- Active Directory Administrative Center is a new GUI tool came with Windows Server 2008 R2, which provides enhanced data management experience to the admin. ADAC helps administrators to perform common Active Directory object management task across multiple domains with the same ADAC instance.

56. ADSIEDIT- Active Directory Service Interfaces Editor is a GUI tool which is used to perform advanced AD object and attribute management. This Active Directory tool helps us to view objects and attributes that are not visible through normal Active Directory Management Consoles. ADSIEDIT can be downloaded and installed along with Windows Server 2003 Support Tools.

57. This is due to domain functional level. If domain functional level of Windows Server 2003 AD is Windows 2000 Mixed, Universal Group option will be grayed out. You need to raise domain functional level to Windows 2000 native or above.

58. ADMT - Active Directory Migration Tool is a tool which is used for migrating Active Directory objects from one domain to another. ADMT is an effective tool that simplifies the process of migrating users, computers, and groups to new domains.

59. When a domain controller is disconnected for a period that is longer than the tombstone life time, one or more objects that are deleted from Active Directory on all other domain controllers may remain on the disconnected domain controller. Such objects are called lingering objects. Lingering objects can be removed from Windows Server 2003 or 2008 using REPADMIN utility.

60. The Global catalog is a container which contains a searchable partial replica of all objects from all domains of the forest, and full replica of all objects from the domain where it is situated. The global catalog is stored on domain controllers that have been designated as global catalog servers and is distributed through multi-master replication.

Global catalogs are mostly used in multi-domain, multisite and complex forest environment, where as Global catalog does not function in a single domain forest.

61. In a forest that contains only a single Active Directory domain, there is no harm in placing both GC and Infrastructure master in same DC, because Infrastructure master does not have any work to do in a single domain environment. But in a forest with multiple and complex domain structure, the infrastructure master should be located on a DC which is not a Global Catalog server. Because the global catalog server holds a partial replica of every object in the forest, the infrastructure master, if placed on a global catalog server, will never update anything, because it does not contain any references to objects that it does not hold.

62. Command line method: nslookupgc._msdcs.<forest root DNS Domain Name>, nltest /dsgetdc:corp /GC. GUI method: Open DNS management, and under 'Forward Lookup Zone', click on GC container. To check if a server is GC or not, go to Active Directory Sites and Services MMC and under 'Servers' folder, take properties of NTDS settings of the desired DC and find Global Catalog option is checked.

63. As per Microsoft, a single AD domain controller can create around 2.15 billion objects during its lifetime.

64. When a user enters a user name and password, the computer sends the user name to the KDC. The KDC contains a master database of unique long term keys for every principal in its realm. The KDC looks up the user's master key (KA), which is based on the user's password. The KDC then creates two items: a session key (SA) to share with the user and a Ticket-Granting Ticket (TGT). The TGT includes a second copy of the SA, the user name, and an expiration time. The KDC encrypts this ticket by using its own master key (KKDC), which only the KDC knows. The client computer receives the information from the KDC and runs the user's password through a one-way hashing function, which converts the password into the user's KA. The client computer now has a session key and a TGT so that it can securely communicate with the KDC. The client is now authenticated to the domain and is ready to access other resources in the domain by using the Kerberos protocol.

65. Lightweight Directory Access Protocol (LDAP) is an Internet standard protocol which is used as a standard protocol for Active Directory functions. It runs directly over TCP, and can be used to access a standalone LDAP directory service or to access a directory service that is back-ended by X.500.

66. Active Directory related files are by default located at %SystemRoot%\ntds folder. NTDS.DIT is the main Active Directory database file. Apart from this other files such as EDB.LOG, EDB.CHK, RES1.LOG, TEMP.EDB etc. are also located at the same folder.

67. Global Catalog servers produce huge traffic related to the replication process. There for making all the domain controllers in the forest as Global Catalog servers will cause network bandwidth problem. GCs should be placed based on Network bandwidth and user or application requirement.

68. Netdomm is used to manage Active Directory domains and trust relationships from the command prompt. Some of the Netdom functions include; Join a computer to domain, Establish one-way or two-way trust relationships between domains, Manage trust relationships between domains, Manages the primary and alternate names for a computer etc.

69. Role seizure is the action of assigning an operations master role to a new domain controller without the support of the existing role holder (generally because it is offline due to a hardware failure). During role seizure, a new domain controller assumes the operations master role without communicating with the existing role holder. Role seizure can be done using repadmin.exe and Ntdsutil.exe commands.

70. Inter-Site Topology Generator. One domain controller per site holds the Inter-Site Topology Generator (ISTG) role, which is responsible for managing the inbound replication connection objects for all bridgehead servers in the site in which it is located.

71. Yes, this is possible using PowerShell command, with the help of LastLogonTimeStamp. Commands and pipes such as Get-ADUser, Where-Object, LastLogonDate etc. can be used to get inactive users.

72. Group Policy allows you to implement specific configurations for users and computers. Group Policy settings are contained in Group Policy objects (GPOs), which are linked to the following Active Directory service containers: sites, domains, or organizational units (OUs).

73. A Group Policy Object (GPO) is a collection of settings that control the working environment of user accounts and computer accounts. GPOs define registry-based policies, security options, software installation and maintenance options, script options, and folder redirection options.

    There are two kinds of Group Policy objects:

    i.   Local Group Policy objects are stored on individual computers.
    ii. Nonlocal Group Policy objects, which are stored on a domain controller, are available only in an Active Directory environment.

74. GPO applies in this order – Local Policy, Site, Domain, and Organizational Units.

75. CSVDE and LDIFDE are used to Import or Export Active Directory data to a file. CSV (comma-separated value) format files can be read with MS Excel and are simply altered with a batch script. LDIF files (LDAP Data Interchange Format) are a cross-platform standard.

76. A user object is an object that is a security principal in the directory. A user can log on to the network with these authorizations and access permissions can be granted to users. A contact object is an account that does not have any security permissions. You cannot log on to the network as a contact. Contacts are normally used to indicate outside users for the purpose of e-mail.

77. A bridgehead server is a domain controller in each site, which is used as a interaction point to obtain and replicate data between sites. For intersite replication, KCC entitles one of the domain controllers as a bridgehead server. In case the server is down, KCC entitles another one from the domain controller. When a bridgehead server obtains

replication updates from another site, it replicates the data to the other domain controllers within its site.

78. Active Directory replication occurs between domain controllers when directory data is updated on one domain controller and that update is replicated to all other domain controllers. When a change in directory data occurs, the source domain controller sends out a notice that its directory store now contains updated data. The domain controller's replication partners then send a request to the source domain controller to receive those updates. Usually, the source domain controller sends out a change notification after a delay. However, any delay in replication can result in a security risk for definite types of changes. Urgent replication ensures that critical directory changes are immediately replicated, including account lockouts, changes in the account lockout policy, changes in the domain password policy, and changes to the password on a domain controller account.

79. Realm trust is a transitive or non-transitive one way or two way trust used to form a trust relationship between a non-Windows Kerberos realm and a Windows Server 2003 domain. This trust relationship allows cross-platform interoperability with security services based on other Kerberos V5 versions such as UNIX and MIT implementations.

80. An Active Directory structure is an arrangement of information about objects. The objects fall into two broad categories: resources (e.g., printers) and security principals (user or computer accounts and groups). Security principals are assigned unique security identifiers (SIDs).Each object represents a single entity—whether a user, a computer, a printer, or a group—and its attributes. Certain objects can contain other objects. An object is uniquely identified by its name and has a set of attributes—the characteristics and information that the object represents— defined by a schema, which also determines the kinds of objects that can be stored in Active Directory.

81. Adding custom attribute involves modification in Active Directory schema which requires the modifying user to be a member of Schema Administrators and Enterprise Administrators groups. By default, the Administrator account is a member of the

Schema Administrator group. You can use adsiedit.msc or schmmgmt.msc to modify the properties of an AD object.

82. When a new domain user or group account is created, Active Directory stores the account's SID in the Object-SID (objectSID) property of a User or Group object. It also allocates the new object a globally unique identifier (GUID), which is a 128-bit value that is unique not only in the enterprise but also across the world. GUIDs are assigned to every object created by Active Directory. Each object's GUID is stored in its Object-GUID (objectGUID) property.

83. Dcpromo

84. Yes. Keeping your Active Directory as simple as possible will help improve overall efficiency, and it will make the troubleshooting process easier whenever problems arise. Use the appropriate site topology. Use dedicated domain controllers. Have at least two DNS servers. Place at least one global catalog server in each site.

85. There are many changes in Active Directory from 2003 version to 2008 version, like Active Directory is a service now that can be restarted. RODC is a new type of DC introduce in windows 2008. Group policy preference mode is introduced. New number of AD templates has been introduced in 2008. DFS is being used for replication instead of FRS in 2003.Windows Server 2008 AD includes new features such as Active Directory Recycle Bin, Active Directory Administrative Center, Active Directory Web Services, Offline domain join etc.

86. In order to configure Windows Server 2008 R2 Domain Controller within Windows 2003 network we need to check if Domain Functional Level is set up at least in Windows 2000 native mode. But preferable Domain Functional Level is Windows Server 2003. When it's set up in Windows Server 2003 mode, and you have only one domain in a forest or each domains have only Windows 2003 Domain Controllers, you are also able to raise Forest Functional Level to Windows Server 2003 to use Read-Only Domain Controller (RODC) within your network.

87. Replication within a site occurs automatically on the basis of change notification. Intrasite replication begins when you make a directory update on a domain controller. By default, the source domain controller waits 15 seconds and then sends an update notification to its closest replication partner. If the source domain controller has more than one replication partner, subsequent notifications go out by default at 3 second intervals to each partner. By default, intersite replication across each site link occurs every 180 minutes (3 hours). You can adjust this frequency to match your specific needs.

88. Open Active Directory Users and Computers. In the console tree, right-click Active Directory Users and Computers, and then click Connect to Domain Controller. In Enter the name of another domain controller, type the name of the domain controller you want to hold the RID master role. In the console tree, right-click Active Directory Users and Computers, point to All Tasks, and then click Operations Masters. Click the RID tab, and then click Change.

89. We can use ntdsutil commands to perform database maintenance of AD DS, manage and control single master operations, Active Directory Backup restoration and remove metadata left behind by domain controllers that were removed from the network without being properly uninstalled.

90. Active Directory Domain Services, Active Directory Web Services, Netlogon Service, Windows Time Service.

91. Immediate impact if PDC Emulator fails. RID master impact only when RID pool finishes. Will not be able to create new domain if domain naming master fails. Last impact will be due to schema master role. Schema extension will not be possible.

92. Active Directory database has a habit of becoming fragmented through normal use. The process of adding and removing objects obviously creates fragmentation. The process of reclaiming lost space in the database due to fragmentation is called Active directory defragmentation. There are two types of defragmentation; offline defragmentation and online defragmentation. To perform offline defragmentation you have to start domain controller in Directory Service Restore Mode and then run ntdsutil command.

93. Online Defragmentation: Active Directory database automatically performs online defragmentation during its normal operation in every 12 hours interval. Offline Defragmentation: this is manually performed by an administrator after taking Domain controller to Directory Services Restore Mode and running ntdsutil command.

94. Active Directory can be uninstalled using dcpromo command. Before uninstalling Active Directory, we have to verify that this domain controller is not the only global catalog and it does not hold an operations master role.

95. Check the network connection on the desktop. Try to ping to the domain controller. Run nslookup and check if name resolution is working. Check Active Directory for the computer account of the desktop. Compare the time settings on the desktop and Domain controller. Remove the desktop from domain and rejoin to domain.

96. Active Directory replication issue can occur due to variety of reasons. For example, DNS issue, network problems, security issues etc. Troubleshooting can start by verifying DNS records. Then remove and recreate Domain Controller replication link. Check the time settings on both replication partners. Command line repadmin and replmon tools can be used to troubleshoot replication issues.

97. Check for any automatic programs or devices which use Exchange actives sync, which will use old password even after user changes the password. Advise the user to reconfigure all the programs and devices which use AD credential. Check and verify any scheduled tasks using old passwords. Verify persistent drive mapping with old password. Disconnect terminal service sessions. Reconfigure account lockout threshold if required; if it is set to very narrow.

98. Check the Network Adapter settings and verify the DNS IP address. Configure proper DNS IP address to lookup the Domain Controller.

99. DFSR (Distributed File System Replication) DNS service, RPC Service etc.

100. Application directory partitions are typically created by the applications that will use them to store and replicate data. For testing and troubleshooting needs, members of the Enterprise Admins group can manually create or manage application directory partitions using the Ntdsutil command-line tool.

101. When checking from System perspective, verify that the Domain Controller in the site where user desktops are located is up and connected. If the users still facing the latency there is a probability of network issue and need to be discussed with the team who works with network.

102. A compilation of Microsoft Active Directory related products are generally described as Identity and Access (IDA) solution. This terminology started when Windows Server 2008 released. IDA includes Active Directory Domain Services (AD DS), Active Directory Lightweight Directory (AD LDS), Active Directory Certificate Services (AD CS), Active Directory Rights Managements Services (AD RMS) etc.

103. To view AD Schema, Firstly you need to register dll. Start-run- regsvr32. Then run schmmgmt.dll. Go to run and type mmc and add the Active Directory Schema Snap in to the mmc.

104. Some of the built in groups are: Administrators, Backup Operators, Account Operators, Remote Desktop Users, Server Operators, and Users etc.

105. Enterprise Admins group is a group that performs only in the forest root domain and members of this group have full administrative control on all domains that are in your forest. Domain Admins group is group that is present in each domain. Members of this group have a full administrative control on the domain.

106. PowerShell scripts can be used to created bulk users. There is an Active Directory User Creation tool by Rich Prescott which is very popular.

Hyper-V

Questions & Answers

Questions:

1. What is virtual machine technology?

2. What is virtual machine technology used for?

3. What is Hyper-V?

4. What is Windows hypervisor?

5. What benefits does Hyper-V offer to customers?

6. Will Microsoft continue to support Linux operating systems with Hyper-V?

7. Can you provide a brief overview of Hyper-V's feature set?

8. How will customers migrate to Hyper-V?

9. Are there tools available to assist in planning for Hyper-V migration?

10. How do users access the Hyper-V?

11. Does Microsoft provide technical support for Hyper-V?

12. What is the list of guests that will be supported on Hyper-V?

13. What are the differences between Hyper-V and Virtual Server?

14. Does running Windows NT in a virtual machine mean that Microsoft is extending its support for the product?

15. What are the system requirements for Hyper-V?

16. How many virtual machines can run per processor?

17. Does Hyper-V support 64-bit processors?

18. Does Hyper-V support symmetric multiprocessing (SMP) in the virtual machine environment?

19. What are the prerequisites to install and use Hyper-V?

20. How Microsoft virtual server manages the virtualization platform?

21. What are the features provided in Microsoft Virtual Server?

22. What are the limitations of Microsoft Virtual server?

23. What are the challenges faced by remote site virtualization?

24. What are the similarities between the Virtual server and physical server?

25. What is the authentication protocol that is used for Microsoft virtual servers?

26. What are the limitations of Kerberos protocol?

27. What are the benefits involved in virtual server host clustering?

28. What is the difference between Host and Guest clustering?

29. What is the difference between Host clustering and standard clustering?

30. What are the steps to be taken to secure Microsoft virtual server?

31. What is the process of creating a virtual network?

32. Define Virtual server architecture.

Answers:

1. Virtual machine technology applies to both server and client hardware. Virtual machine technology enables multiple operating systems to run concurrently on a single machine. In particular, Hyper-V, a key feature of Windows Server 2012, enables one or more operating systems to run simultaneously on the same physical system. Today, many operating systems are supported by Virtual PC 2007, Virtual Server 2005, and Hyper-V.

2. Virtual machine technology serves a variety of purposes. It enables hardware consolidation, because multiple operating systems can run on one computer. Key applications for virtual machine technology include cross-platform integration.

3. Hyper-V, previously codenamed Viridian, is a hypervisor-based technology that is a key feature of Windows Server 2012. It provides a scalable, reliable, and highly available virtualization platform. It is part of Microsoft's ongoing effort to provide our customers and partners with the best operating system platform for virtualization.

4. A core component of Hyper-V, Windows hypervisor is a thin layer of software between the hardware and the OS that allows multiple operating systems to run, unmodified, on a host computer at the same time. It provides simple partitioning functionality and is responsible for maintaining strong isolation between partitions. It has an inherently secure architecture with minimal attack surface, as it does not contain any third-party device drivers.

5. Hyper-V provides customers an ideal platform for key virtualization scenarios, such as production server consolidation, business continuity management, software test and development, and development of a dynamic datacenter. Hyper-V provides key functionality, which an ideal virtualization platform should provide—scalability, high performance, reliability, security, flexibility, and manageability. It provides scalability and high performance by supporting features like guest multi-processing support and 64-bit guest and host support; reliability and security through its hypervisor architecture; flexibility and manageability by supporting features like quick migration of

virtual machines from one physical host to another, and integration with System Center Virtual Machine Manager.

6. Yes, Microsoft provides integration components and technical support for customers running select Linux distributions as guest operating systems within Hyper-V. Please check the Supported Guest Operating Systems page for more information and updates.

7. Some of the capabilities of Hyper-V include x64 host and guest support, ability to run guest machines in a multi-processor environment, large memory allocation per virtual machine, integrated virtual switch support, and ability to migrate virtual machines across hosts with minimal downtime. With the R2 release of Hyper-V, Live Migration, new processor support, and dynamic virtual machine capabilities were added.

8. Customers who invest in the .vhd file format—the format used by Virtual Server, as well as a multitude of vendor licensees—will have a clear path forward to Hyper-V. Customers can leverage V2V capabilities in System Center Virtual Machine Manager to conveniently migrate from Virtual Server or VMware to Hyper-V or work with Microsoft's partners who provide migration solutions.

9. Yes, the Microsoft Assessment and Planning (MAP) Toolkit helps you plan for Hyper-V migration by determining which of your physical servers are underutilized and, therefore, good candidates for server virtualization.

10. Users can go to Server Manager and install the Hyper-V role. After the Hyper-V role is enabled, Hyper-V Manager will become available as a part of Administrative Tools. From the Hyper-V Manager users can easily create and configure virtual machines.

11. Yes, technical support for Hyper-V is part of the support for Windows Server 2012. For more information on support, please refer to the Windows Server 2012 Support page.

12. Microsoft supports a number of guest OS environments including Windows Server 2008 R2, Windows Server 2008, Windows Server 2003, Windows 2000 Server, Windows 7, Windows Vista, Windows XP and Novell SUSE.

13. Microsoft Virtual Server 2005 R2 is the current server virtualization solution from Microsoft and is based on a hosted virtualization platform. Hyper-V, a key feature of Windows Server 2012, is a hypervisor-based virtualization platform that will enable

customers to not only consolidate a vast array of workloads but also enable moving toward a dynamic IT environment. Core feature set differences include support for 64 guest virtual machines, SMP support, performance improvements, and other key features in Hyper-V.

14. No. While you may receive benefit from moving the applications from physical hardware to virtual machines, running applications in a virtual environment does not extend their support life cycles. For more information about the support life-cycle timeframes.

15. In addition to the systems requirement for Windows Server 2012, the two key requirements for the Hyper-V platform are the need to ensure that the server is a 64-bit environment and supports hardware-assisted virtualization (Intel VT or AMD-V) technology.

16. The number of virtual machines running per host depends on many factors, including physical memory, processor, and workload running in the guest. With Hyper-V, you define the amount of memory available to a virtual machine, and that memory allocation can be altered to reflect the needs of the virtual machine.

17. Hyper-V runs on a 64-bit (x64) server platform and requires support of either AMD64 or Intel IA-32e/EM64T (x64) processors with hardware-assisted virtualization support. Note that Hyper-V does not support Itanium (IA-64) processors. For the virtual machines, Hyper-V supports both 32-bit and 64-bit systems as guest OSes.

18. Hyper-V supports both uniprocessor and multiprocessor configurations in the virtual machine environment.

19. In addition to the system requirements for Windows Server 2012 as described in the release notes, a 64-bit system with hardware-assisted virtualization enabled and data execution prevention (DEP) is required. It is also recommended to ensure that you have a clean install of x64 edition of Windows Server 2012 to be able to use the Hyper-V technology.

20. Microsoft virtual server provides virtualization platform that allows the creation of virtual machine using a windows operating system. It is developed by Connectix.

This platform provides the provision to create and manage the virtual machines using IIS web based interface that keeps all the settings and configuration at one place. It also allows the management of network configuration for communicating with host operating system or other guest operating systems.

21. Microsoft Virtual server includes the following features:

    - It includes the support for Linux guest operating system.

    - It includes Virtual Disk pre-compactor tool that prepares the disk for compacting.

    - It includes SMP (Symmetric multiprocessing) for the host operating system.

    - It includes the mounting feature for virtual hard drives on host operating system that enables backups to be taken.

    - It includes the tool to mount VHD images.

22. The limitations of Microsoft Virtual server includes:

    - It doesn't support 64 bit processors and can't run 64 bit guests.

    - It uses SMP but doesn't have virtualization in it.

    - It has limitation for guest users to use not more than one CPU.

    - It decreases the performance of the system as the instruction set also get virtualized which increases the overhead on the application.

    - It has very limited interaction with the host hardware.

23. Remote site virtualization provides server virtualization and need for remote management for the virtual machines. It is provided due to limited resources that might not exist. The main challenge is to apply the server consolidations. Each server is using dedicative service functions and small servers and not using multiple servers. If single server approach is being given then there will be less power requirements, space requirements and only one server to manage and backup that will make it prone to fail and reduce the efficiency.

24. The virtual server provided by Microsoft and physical server has few things common in between them and these are as follows:

- Both allow access to network resources that has to be shared between two computers.

- Both publish the resources to the network clients under a unique server name.

- Both are under same network name and IP address range.

- Both are used to provide same communication option.

- Both provide the same networking modes of operations through which clients can communicate with each other.

25. Kerberos is the authentication protocol that is being used by virtual servers. It maintains an active directory computer object that is involved in clustering. This provides the client security and easy to use features. It provides the provision of message queuing on a virtual server and allows the clients to publish the information to other computer systems. It provides clustering as well and by configuring its properties more options can be found out to be used.

26. The limitations of Kerberos protocol that is being used by the Microsoft virtual server are as follows:

- There is no provision to apply group policies to virtual server. This means that there is no provision to apply policies on the applications that are running on virtual server. Virtual server object can't define group policies using this protocol.

- Kerberos protocol provides clustering option but it is limited to a certain server computer object. This object is being managed by active directory by default.

- There is no provision to rename a network name resource and change the configuration of kerberos authentication at same time. As the actions will be performed the changes will automatically be reflected on it.

27. The benefits that are involved in virtual server host clustering are as follows:

- Server consolidation: Allow virtual servers to consolidate multiple servers into one that will be easy to track and maintain virtual machines at one server together.

- Increased availability: Virtual server host clustering increases the availability of consolidated server due to which if any failure occurs then another server can take up the job that is being served by the first server. The effect of failure is kept to minimum by providing risk management systems.

28. Host clustering keeps the physical host as cluster node and if host stops performing then the processes can be given to another host to run, whereas guest clustering keeps the guest as cluster node and if guest stops working then it will fail all other guest that are connected with it.

Host clustering protects from failure of the computer that is crashed, whereas guest clustering doesn't provide protection from failure.

29. Host clustering protects system from failure due to the fact that guests are configured as clustered resource group and I consists of generic script resource, whereas standard clustering provide automatic checks to discover the cause of the failure and recover from it.

Host clustering doesn't monitor the cluster services, whereas standard clustering monitors the failure.

30. To secure Microsoft the virtual server the steps that are required are as follows:

- The configuration file of virtual server services has to be secured.
- Individual files that contain the configuration files and resources that are associated with the virtual server have to be secured.
- IIS (Internet information services) has to be secured with the administration website to secure the virtual platform and the virtual machines.
- Virtual server is configured securely such as the security breaches are lower in number as it only allows those members that are directly associated with the local administrators. The permissions are given to those who are associated with it. Virtual network configuration file has to be secured to save the further transmission over the web and between different systems.

31. To create a virtual network virtual machines are required that has to be configured for the accessing. Virtual network is supported by virtual server to connect many virtual machines that can be shared with many computers in the network. Virtual network require network adapter to be configured and installed to a physical computer, this way any computer can access the resources from any other computer. Virtual server uses DHCP server to dynamically assign the IP address to the computer systems so that they can connect with other systems. Virtual server in this case has virtual DHCP that allows system to be uniquely identified.

   Multiple Virtual network can be configured on a single network adapter by creating and associating the virtual network with a network adapter. After the steps virtual machines can be added to the virtual network of host operating system.

32. Virtual server consists of virtual network that in turn consists of virtual machines. It allows traffic to be isolated in virtual network while communicating with the host operating system. It allows the handling of network devices by virtual machine network service driver. This virtual machine network service driver come with the virtual server setup that is being performed on the host operating system. The main function of the network driver is to monitor the traffic and the routing packets. The virtual network can have several options defined like:

   - It is not attached to physical network adapter.
   - It can attach to dedicated physical network adapter.
   - More than one network can attach to same physical network adapter.
   - Virtual machines are attached to same virtual network.

References

- All Technical Interview Questions & Answers, Available at:

   http://www.01world.in/p/vmware-admin-interview-questions.html(Accessed: 4th
   October 2014).

- AnasTechspot (2012) Active Directory Interview Questions and Answers, Available at:

   http://www.anas.co.in/2012/03/active-directory-interview-questions.html(Accessed:
   16th August 2014).

- Best Features of Windows Server 2012, Available at:

   http://www.theregister.co.uk/2013/01/10/10_best_server12/ (Accessed: 6th September
   2014).

- Carvalho, L. (2012) Windows Server 2012 Hyper-V Cookbook, 1st ed. UK: Packt Publishing
   Ltd.

- Difference between Windows Server 2008 R2 and Windows Server 2012, Available at:

   http://www.learnmsexchange.com/windows-servers/windows-server-2012/625-
   difference-between-windows-server-2008-r2-and-windows-server-2012   (Accessed:
   4[th]May 2014).

- Eli the Computer Guy (2013) FREECOPIERSUPPORT: WINDOWS SERVER 2012 [Online].
   Available at:
   https://www.youtube.com/watch?v=F7JJX9rLqsw&list=PLIkz4IIG40a61wCh1UFEOeReqZ
   PLI_R8U (Accessed: 8[th]March 2014).

- Gajengi, V. (2011) Group Policy Interview Questions, Available at:

http://vajramg.blogspot.in/2011/04/group-policy-interview-questions.html(Accessed: 15[th]November 2014).

- Hassell, J. (2012) 10 Key Windows Server 2012 Features for IT Pros. Available at: http://www.cio.com/article/2393205/servers/10-key-windows-server-2012-features-for-it-pros.html(Accessed: 5[th]April 2014).

- Johnson, M.S. (2012) The Storage Team at Microsoft – File Cabinet Blog. Available at: http://blogs.technet.com/b/filecab/archive/2012/05/21/introduction-to-data-deduplication-in-windows-server-2012.aspx (Accessed: 4th May 2014).

- Key Advantages of Windows Server 2012, Available at: http://windowsserver2012.itpro.co.uk/business-benefits/26/12-key-advantages-windows-server-2012/page/0/2(Accessed: 25[th]April 2014).

- Kumar, R. (2012) Important interview questions and answers, Available at: http://pokhnet.blogspot.in/2012/10/important-interview-questians.html(Accessed: 27[th]October 2014).

- Lynn, S. (2012) Windows Server 2012: Up and Running 1st ed. Sebastopol: O'Reilly Media, Inc.

- Mackin, C. J. and Thomas, O. (2014) Configuring Advanced Windows Server 2012 services 1st ed. USA: One Microsoft Way.

- Microsoft virtual server interview questions and answers, Available at: http://careerride.com/microsoft-virtual-server-interview-questions.aspx(Accessed: 12[th]November 2014).

- Moran, J. (No Date) SkillSoft Course: IT Professionals Certifications [Online]. Available at: http://acm.skillport.com/skillportfe/main.action?content=catalog(Accessed: 9th March 2014).

- Morimoto, R. et al. (2013) Windows Server 2012 Unleashed 1st ed. USA: Pearson Education, Inc.

- Otey, M. (2011) Top 10: New Features in Windows Server 2012, Available at: http://windowsitpro.com/windows-server-2012/top-10-new-features-windows-server-2012(Accessed: 19th May 2014).

- Panek, W. (2013) Windows Server 2012: Complete Study Guide 1st ed. Indiana: Wilky& Sons, Inc.

- Pathak, A (2012) Hyper-V Questions and answers, Available at: http://ankurpathakniit.blogspot.in/2012/09/hyper-v-questions-and-answers.html(Accessed: 11th October2014).

- Stanek, R. W. (2012) Windows Server 2012 Pocket Consultant 1st ed. USA: One Microsoft Way.

- Sujit, S. (2008) Interview Based Question AD DNS FSMO GPO, Available at: http://www.scribd.com/doc/6240894/Interview-Based-Question-AD-DNS-FSMO-GPO#scribd(Accessed: 13th September2014).

- Thind, J. (2012) Server 2012 Training Videos in Hindi [Online]. Available at: https://www.youtube.com/watch?v=uHysTrGlhYI&list=PLks8W396lro635rX6F1P4AckMt0OTGGIV(Accessed: 25th March 2014).

- Tulloch, M. (2012) Introducing Windos Server 2012 1st ed. USA: One Microsoft Way.

- Vashisht, N (2014) Top Interview Questions for System Administrators (Microsoft), Available at:http://resources.intenseschool.com/top-interview-questions-for-system-administrators-microsoft/(Accessed: 15thDecember 2014).

- Wiley, J. (2013) Administering Windows Server 2012 1st ed. Garamond: Aptara, Inc.

- Zacker, C. (2012) Installing and Configuring Windows Server 2012 3rd ed. USA: One Microsoft Way.